11+

MATHS

Book Six

Stephen C. Curran

This book belongs to:

....

_____

Accelerated Education Publications Ltd.

Contents

Chapter Twenty
ALGEBRA
1. Number Operations
a. The Commutative Rule

A Commutative Operation is where the order of the sum can be changed and it will still give the same answer:

Example: | Demonstrate a Commutative Operation:

$$3 + 5 = 8 \longrightarrow 5 + 3 = 8$$

3 and **5** can be reversed, but still add up to **8**. The Operation is Commutative.

Example: | Are all Operations with **2** and **4** Commutative?

$2 + 4 = 6 \longrightarrow 4 + 2 = 6$
$2 \times 4 = 8 \longrightarrow 4 \times 2 = 8$

Addition and Multiplication are Commutative.

$4 - 2 = 2 \longrightarrow 2 - 4 = -2$
$4 \div 2 = 2 \longrightarrow 2 \div 4 = 0.5$

Subtraction and Division are <u>not</u> Commutative.

Exercise 20: 1 Commutative? Write Yes or No.

1) $3 - 7$ ....   2) 9×3 ....   3) $5 + 8 =$ ....

4) $6 \div 2$ ....   5) 4×7 ....   6) $5 \div 8 =$ ....

7) $7 - 5$ ....   8) $8 \div 2$ .... 9) $3 + 2 =$ ....

10) $9 - 2$ ....   **Mark Out of Ten** $\longrightarrow$ ☐

b. Directed Numbers

The term Directed Numbers is used of numbers when their Positive or Negative signs matter. (See **Book 1, pp. 33-35**)

> **Positive Numbers** (+) are greater than zero. A number with no sign in front of it is known as a Positive Number. **Negative Numbers** (−) are less than zero. All Negative Numbers must have a Negative sign in front of them.

c. Adding and Subtracting

Straightforward Adding and Subtracting takes place along the number line. Remember: Count gaps not numbers.

Examples: | What is **7** take away **10**? (Answer) **-3**

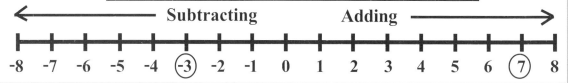

There are some additional rules that need to be understood: If two signs **between** Directed Numbers **meet each other** they are replaced by one sign. It can be summed up as: When signs are the **Same** the result is always **Positive** (+) When signs are **Different** the result is always **Negative** (−)

Positive (+) and **Negative** (−)	$\longrightarrow$	**Negative** (−)
Negative (−) and **Positive** (+)	$\longrightarrow$	**Negative** (−)
Positive (+) and **Positive** (+)	$\longrightarrow$	**Positive** (+)
Negative (−) and **Negative** (−)	$\longrightarrow$	**Positive** (+)

Example: | Show Directed Number Combinations of **3 & 4**:

$$+3 + {^+4} = 3 + 4 = 7 \qquad +3 + {^-4} = 3 - 4 = -1$$
$$+3 - {^-4} = 3 + 4 = 7 \qquad +3 - {^+4} = 3 - 4 = -1$$
$$-3 + {^+4} = -3 + 4 = 1 \qquad -3 + {^-4} = -3 - 4 = -7$$
$$-3 - {^-4} = -3 + 4 = 1 \qquad -3 - {^+4} = -3 - 4 = -7$$

Exercise 20: 2   Calculate the following:

1) **+9 + +5** = ...   2) **-5 + -8** = ...

4

3) $+3 - {}^-7 =$ ....   4) $-6 - {}^-2 =$ ....

5) $+1 - {}^+4 =$ ....   6) $+4 + {}^-7 =$ ....

Remember: Digits with no signs are Positive.

7) $-2 - 3 =$ ....   8) $-4 + 9 =$ ....

9) $1 - {}^-6 =$ ....   10) $6 + 9 =$ ....

d. Multiplying and Dividing

The following rules also apply for Multiplying & Dividing:
When signs are the **Same** the result is always **Positive** (+)
When signs are **Different** the result is always **Negative** (−)

+	×	−	→	−	+	÷	−	→	−
−	×	+	→	−	−	÷	+	→	−
+	×	+	→	+	+	÷	+	→	+
−	×	−	→	+	−	÷	−	→	+

Example: | Show Directed Number Combinations of **2, 3 & 6**

$+2 \times {}^-3 = 2 \times {}^-3 = {}^-6$	$+6 \div {}^-3 = 6 \div {}^-3 = -2$
$-2 \times {}^+3 = -2 \times 3 = {}^-6$	$-6 \div {}^+3 = -6 \div 3 = -2$
$+2 \times {}^+3 = 2 \times 3 = 6$	$+6 \div {}^+3 = 6 \div 3 = 2$
$-2 \times {}^-3 = 2 \times 3 = 6$	$-6 \div {}^-3 = 6 \div 3 = 2$

Exercise 20: 3   Calculate the following:

1) $-4 \times -3 =$ ....   2) $+9 \div -3 =$ ....

3) $-8 \div -2 =$ ....   4) $+9 \times -5 =$ ....

5) $+7 \times +3 =$ ....   6) $+4 \div -2 =$ ....

7) $6 \times 9 =$ ....   8) $-12 \div 6 =$ ....

9) $-16 \div 4 =$ ....   10) $-8 \times 7 =$ ....

2. Order of Operations
a. Brackets for Separation

Brackets ( ) are used (in pairs) to enclose an Operation that is to be treated as one complete quantity and evaluated first.

Example: | Show **2 × 5 + 4** with Brackets and **Solve** the sum:

$$(2 \times 5) + 4 \longrightarrow \text{The Bracket is done first and then the Addition} \quad 10 + 4 = 14$$

To indicate the **Order of Operations** Brackets are used. Multiplications and Divisions are often Bracketed to show that they must be completed first.

Example: | Show **6 × 3 + 4 × 5** in a Bracketed form:

$$(6 \times 3) + (4 \times 5) = 18 + 20 = 38$$

Ignoring the Brackets will lead to an incorrect Order of Operations and totally wrong answers.

$$6 \times 3 + 4 \times 5 = 18 + 4 \times 5 = 22 \times 5 = 110 \text{ (Wrong)}$$

Exercise 20: 4   Calculate the following:

1) **(-5 × 7) − 4**
= ....

2) **(6 × 9) + 9**
= ....

3) **8 + (-5 − -2)**
= ....

4) **(4 ÷ -2) × 3**
= ....

5) **(-4 × -2) + 10**
= ....

6) **(-2 + 9) − 8**
= ....

7) **(-12 ÷ -3) × (-8 × 7)** = ...

8) **(-8 − 4) + (16 ÷ -4)** = ...

9) $(-16 \div 4) + (3 \times 2) = $ .... ☐

10) $(-8 \div -2) \div (4 - 2) = $ ....

b. The Associative Rule

A group of quantities connected by **Repeated** Operators will give the same result if their order stays the same. It will not matter how they are grouped (Bracketed).

Example: | Demonstrate the Associative Rule with $3 \times 4 \times 5$:

$$(5 \times 3) \times 4 = 60 \longrightarrow 3 \times (4 \times 5) = 60$$

The numbers **3**, **4** and **5** in this Multiplication can be paired (Bracketed) in different ways but will always give the answer **60**. The Operation is Associative.

Example: | Show the Associative Rule with **8**, **4** and **2**:

$(8 + 4) + 2 = 14 \longrightarrow 8 + (4 + 2) = 14$	**Addition and Multiplication are Associative.**
$(8 \times 4) \times 2 = 64 \longrightarrow 8 \times (4 \times 2) = 64$	
$(8 \div 4) \div 2 = 1 \longrightarrow 8 \div (4 \div 2) = 4$	**Subtraction and Division are not Associative.**
$(8 - 4) - 2 = 2 \longrightarrow 8 - (4 - 2) = 6$	

c. The Distributive Rule

The **Distributive Rule** of arithmetic says that Multiplication is Distributed over Addition.

Example: | Demonstrate the Distributive Rule with: $2 \times (3 + 5)$

$$2 \times (3 + 5) \longrightarrow 6 + 10 = 16$$

$(2 \times 3) + (2 \times 5)$

The **3** and the **5** within the Bracket is Multiplied by the **2** outside the Bracket.

7

d. Brackets for Multiplication

If two numbers are Multiplied by the same number the standard way of representing it is with two Brackets:

Example: | Show $4 \times 3 + 4 \times 5$ in Bracketed form.

$$(4 \times 3) + (4 \times 5)$$

This type of Bracketed expression can be shown more **simply** by using only one Bracket. **Everything inside the Bracket is Multiplied by everything outside the Bracket**.

Example: | Show $(4 \times 3) + (4 \times 5)$ with one Bracket only.

$$4(3 + 5)$$

The **Distributive Rule** is applied here - Multiplication is distributed over Addition (Multiplication is applied to each of the added numbers in the Bracket). The Bracket is **Expanded** or **Solved** by Multiplying out the numbers.

Example: | Expand or Solve the sum $4(3 + 5)$.

$(4 \times 3) + (4 \times 5)$
$$12 + 20 = 32$$

If the number outside the bracket is **Negative**, all the signs of the terms inside the Bracket are changed:

Example: | Expand the sum. $-2(4 + 5)$

$(-2 \times 4) + (-2 \times 5)$
$$-8 - 10 = -18$$

Brackets can result in Squared Numbers:

Example: | Expand the sum. $3(3 + 4)$

$$3^2 + 12 = 9 + 12$$
$(3 \times 3) + (3 \times 4)$
$$= 21$$

A Squared Bracket means all its contents are Squared:

Example: | Expand the sum. $(1 + 4)^2$

$$(5)^2 = 5 \times 5$$
$$= 25$$

A Squared Negative number always gives a Positive answer:

Example: | Expand the sum. $(1 - 6)^2$ |

$(-5)^2 = -5 \times -5$
$= 25$

Exercise 20: 5 — Put these sums into **Single Brackets**:

1) -3×-3

$= \ldots\ldots\ldots\ldots$

2) $(2 \times 3) + (2 \times 4)$

$= \ldots\ldots\ldots\ldots\ldots\ldots$

3) $(5 \times -3) + (5 \times 7)$

$= \ldots\ldots\ldots\ldots\ldots$

4) $4^2 + 20$

$= \ldots\ldots\ldots\ldots$

Expand, then **Solve** the Bracketed expressions:

5) $3(3 - -5) = \ldots\ldots\ldots\ldots\ldots\ldots = \ldots\ldots\ldots$

6) $-3(5 + 2) = \ldots\ldots\ldots\ldots\ldots\ldots = \ldots\ldots\ldots$

7) $-7(-5 + -2) = \ldots\ldots\ldots\ldots\ldots\ldots = \ldots\ldots\ldots$

Give the **Solutions** to these Bracketed sums:

8) $5(5 - 3)$

9) $(5 + 2)^2$

10) $6(3 + 6)$

$= \ldots\ldots\ldots$ $= \ldots\ldots\ldots$ $= \ldots\ldots\ldots$

e. BODMAS

BODMAS is an acronym which helps to remind us about the Order certain Operations have to follow:

B O D M A S

Brackets **O**ver **D**ivide, **M**ultiply, **A**dd, **S**ubtract
(take priority)

Order of Operations is as follows:

First - Do anything in **Brackets**.

Second - Do any **Dividing** then **Multiplying**.

Third - Do any **Adding** then **Subtracting**.

Example: | Work out the following sum using BODMAS:

$$\frac{30}{(4+2)} \times (1 + 2 \times 3)^2 - 4$$

1.a. Work out the **Brackets** first:
$$(4 + 2) = \underline{6}$$

1.b. **BODMAS** applies within the Brackets. <u>Multiply</u>, <u>Add</u> and then <u>Square</u>:
$$(1 + 2 \times 3)^2$$
$$2 \times 3 = 6 + 1 = 7^2 = \underline{49}$$

$$\frac{30}{6} \times 49 - 4$$

$$5 \times 49 - 4$$

2. Next work out the **Division** and then the **Multiplication**:
$$30 \div 6 = \underline{5}; \quad 5 \times 49 = \underline{245}$$

$$245 - 4$$

3. Now do the **Subtraction**:
$$245 - 4 = \underline{241}$$

241 (answer)

Exercise 20: 6   Calculate the following:

1) $(22 - 3) \times 5 + 4$

= ....

2) The two sums are treated as Bracketed

$$\frac{50 - 2}{\text{-}4 \times 2} \longrightarrow \frac{(50 - 2)}{(\text{-}4 \times 2)}$$

= ....

3) $(10 \times 12) + (2 \times \text{-}5)^2$

= ....

4) $2(2 + \text{-}3) + 2$

= ....

5) $(3 \times 6) + (\text{-}1 \times \text{-}5) + (3 \times 1)^2 = $ ....

6) $\text{-}4(\text{-}5 + 2) - 6$

= ....

7) $(7^2 + 2^2) - (4 - 1)^2$

= ....

8) $4(\text{-}2 - 2) + (\text{-}3 - 5) + (3 \times 2)^2 = $ ....

9) $\dfrac{(3 \times \text{-}5)}{(6 - 9)} + 10 = $ ....

10) $20 - 5(\text{-}3 + 2)$

= ....

10

3. Arithmetic Equations

Equations are mathematical sentences or number sentences that always follow the same pattern. What is on the left side is **Balanced** or **Equal to** what is on the right side. This is always signified by an **Equals Sign**.

Examples: | Show Equations using the Four Rules of Number:

Both Equations remain balanced giving the same answer on each side.

$$7 - 3 = 1 + 3 \qquad 2 \times 3 = 12 \div 2$$
$$4 = 4 \qquad\qquad 6 = 6$$

a. Missing Numbers

The Equals Sign permits a Missing Number to be found. **Inverse Operations** can be used to solve the Equations. Remember: **+ is the Inverse of −** and **× is the Inverse of ÷**

Examples: | Find the missing numbers in these Equations:

$\boxed{?} + 6 = 13$ The number in the box is **7** because: $\boxed{7} + 6 = 13$ (inverted $\boxed{7} = 13 - 6$)

$6 \times \boxed{?} = 18$ The number in the box is **3** because: $6 \times \boxed{3} = 18$ (inverted $\boxed{3} = 18 \div 6$)

Exercise 20: 7   Calculate the following:

1) $50 - \boxed{} = 31$ 2) $76 + 35 = 82 + \boxed{}$

3) $(56 \div 7) - 4 = \boxed{} - 24$ 4) $\boxed{} + 5 = 26$

5) $(\text{-}5 \times \text{-}7) + 9 = (36 \div \boxed{}) + 40$

6) $129 - 50 = \boxed{} - 6$ 7) $\boxed{} + 16 = 39 + 8$

8) $(12 \times \text{-}7) + 83 = (8 \times 10) - \boxed{}$

9) $(7 \times \boxed{}) + 5 = 25 + (2 \times 11)$

10) $(6 \times 7) + (4 \times 3) = (7 \times 4) + \boxed{}$ $\boxed{\text{mark}}$

b. Missing Signs

The Equals Sign permits a Missing Operation to be found.
Test different signs to find the correct Operation:

Example: $\boxed{\text{Find the missing Operation in this Equation:}}$

$9 \boxed{?} 5 = 14$ The Operation in the box is + because:

$9 \boxed{+} 5 = 14$ (Check it with the $14 - 5 = 9$
Inverse Operations) $14 - 9 = 5$

Exercise 20: 8   Calculate the following: $\boxed{}$

1) $40 \boxed{} 9 = 31$ 2) $13 + 35 = 12 \boxed{} 4$

3) $(32 \div 4) - 4 = 28 \boxed{} 24$ 4) $57 \boxed{} 3 = 19$

5) $12 \times 6 = 96 \boxed{} 24$ 6) $3 \times 17 = 100 \boxed{} 49$

7) $33 - 17 = 4 \boxed{} 12$ 8) $21 \div 3 = 84 \boxed{} 12$

9) $5(5 + 3) + 100 = 100 + 30 + (40 \boxed{} 4)$

10) $(6 \times 3) \boxed{} 6 = 13 + 43 + 63 - 11$

4. Function Machines

Function Machines (also known as Number Machines or Mappings - see **Book 5**, **p.54**) are Equations.

Example: | How do Function Machines relate to Equations? |

Input Value
(a Number goes
into the Machine)

Operations
(Add, Subtract,
Multiply, Divide)

Output Value
(a Number comes
out of the Machine)

Any Input
Value can
be placed
in the
Function
Machine.

IN   **OPERATION**   **OUT**

$$36 \rightarrow \boxed{\div\ 3} \rightarrow 12$$

$$36 \div 3 = 12$$

The Output Value is
Equal to the Input
Value with the
Operational process
acting on it. This
means the Function
Machine can be
viewed as an **Equation**.

a. Finding Output Values

Output Values are discovered by applying the Order of Operations in the Function Machine:

Example: | Find the Output Value of the Machine. |

IN   **OPERATION**   **OUT**

$$6 \rightarrow \boxed{\times\ 2\ +\ 4} \rightarrow \dots?\dots$$

Multiply by **2** and Add **4**

This machine has more
than one Operation:
$6 \times 2 = 12$ $12 + 4 = 16$

The Output Value = 16

Tables can show the results
of a Function Machine.
Different amounts can be fed
into the same Function
Machine with the following
results:

In	Out
12 ⟶	28
16 ⟶	36
20 ⟶	44
24 ⟶	52

Exercise 20: 9   Calculate the following:

1) $24 \rightarrow \boxed{\div 3} \rightarrow$ ......   2) $3 \rightarrow \boxed{\times 9 - 7} \rightarrow$ ......

3) $57 \rightarrow \boxed{\div 3 - \text{-}7} \rightarrow$ ......   4) $33 \rightarrow \boxed{\times 5} \rightarrow$ ......

Fill in the Function Machine before calculating:

5) $20 \rightarrow \boxed{} \rightarrow$ ......   6) $11 \rightarrow \boxed{} \rightarrow$ ......

Multiply by **9** and Subtract **18**.   Add **15** and Divide by **2**.

7) $8 \rightarrow \boxed{- 3 \times 13} \rightarrow$ ......

8-10) Use the Operations $- 3 \times 13$ in this Function Machine to calculate the three Output Values in the table:

In	Out
-4	....
6	....
11	....

b. Finding Input Values

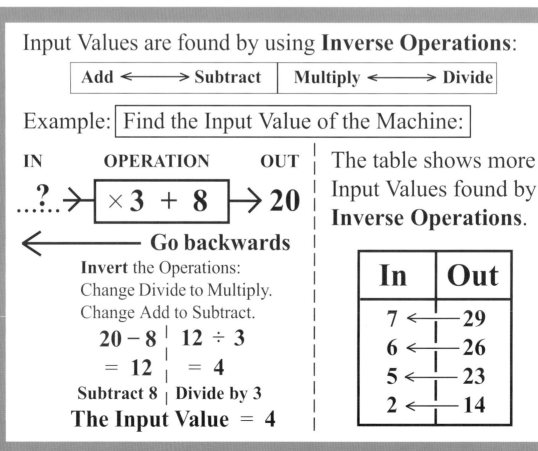

Input Values are found by using **Inverse Operations**:

Add $\longleftrightarrow$ Subtract	Multiply $\longleftrightarrow$ Divide

Example: | Find the Input Value of the Machine: |

IN   OPERATION   OUT

$...\overset{?}{...} \rightarrow \boxed{\times 3 + 8} \rightarrow 20$

$\longleftarrow$ **Go backwards**

Invert the Operations:
Change Divide to Multiply.
Change Add to Subtract.

$20 - 8$	$12 \div 3$
$= 12$	$= 4$
Subtract 8	Divide by 3

The Input Value $= 4$

The table shows more Input Values found by **Inverse Operations**.

In	Out
7 $\longleftarrow$	29
6 $\longleftarrow$	26
5 $\longleftarrow$	23
2 $\longleftarrow$	14

Exercise 20: 10 — Calculate the following:

1) $\dots\dots \rightarrow \boxed{\div\ 5} \rightarrow 75$ 2) $\dots\dots \rightarrow \boxed{\times\ 9 + 9} \rightarrow 90$

3) $\dots\dots \rightarrow \boxed{\times\ 3 + 3} \rightarrow 63$ 4) $\dots\dots \rightarrow \boxed{\times\ 4} \rightarrow 96$

Fill in the Function Machine before calculating:

5) $\dots\dots \rightarrow \boxed{} \rightarrow 76$ 6) $\dots\dots \rightarrow \boxed{} \rightarrow 91$

Multiply by **4** and Add **20**.   Multiply by **5** and Add **16**.

7) $\dots\dots \rightarrow \boxed{-\ 2 \times 11} \rightarrow 44$

8-10) Use the Operations $-\ 2 \times 11$ in this Function Machine to calculate the Input Values in the table:

In	Out
....	66
....	88
....	132

c. Finding Number Operations

A Missing Operation is found by guessing and testing. Try the Operations $\boxed{+\ -\ \times\ \div}$ in the Function Machine:

Example: $\boxed{\text{Find the missing Operation in the Machine.}}$

- As the number is increasing we do not Divide or Subtract.
- We cannot Multiply since there is no Multiple that will increase 54 to 99.
- We must **Add**. The answer can be found by Inverting the Operation to Subtract.

IN   OPERATION   OUT

$9 \rightarrow \boxed{\times\ 6 \quad \boxed{?}} \rightarrow 99$

Multiply by **6** and **?**

Calculate the first Operation. | To find the **Add**, Invert and Subtract.

$9 \times 6 = 54$ | $99 - 54 = 45$

$54 \boxed{+}\ 45 = 99$

The Missing Operation is $\boxed{\text{Add 45}}$

15

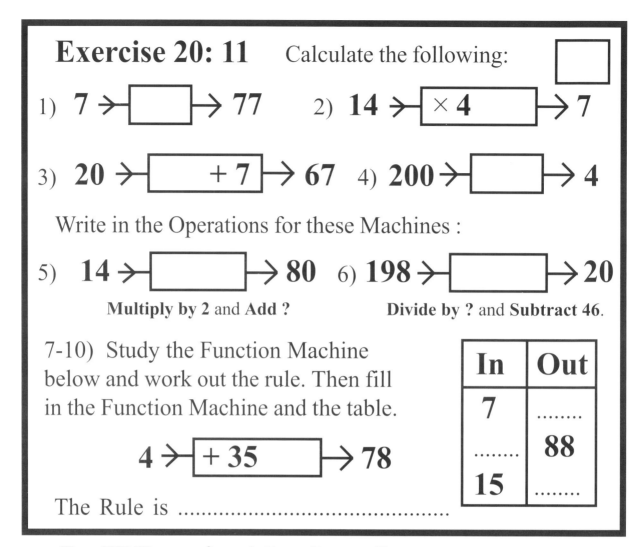

Exercise 20:11   Calculate the following:

1) 7 ⇾ [ ] ⇾ 77   2) 14 ⇾ [× 4] ⇾ 7

3) 20 ⇾ [+ 7] ⇾ 67   4) 200 ⇾ [ ] ⇾ 4

Write in the Operations for these Machines :

5) 14 ⇾ [ ] ⇾ 80   6) 198 ⇾ [ ] ⇾ 20

Multiply by 2 and **Add ?**   **Divide by ?** and **Subtract 46.**

7-10) Study the Function Machine below and work out the rule. Then fill in the Function Machine and the table.

4 ⇾ [+ 35] ⇾ 78

In	Out
7	....
....	88
15	....

The Rule is ....

5. What is Algebra?

In Algebra letters or symbols represent **Missing Numbers**. Italicised lower case letters are normally used from the beginning or end of the alphabet. They are called **Variables**.

Example: | What letters are mostly used in Algebra? |

a, b, c, and x, y, z.

A **Constant** is a Value that remains unchanged. It is usually a number. **Terms** are quantities (Constants and/or Variables) that are linked by + or − signs.

Example: | Show a Constant and Variable as Terms: |

Variable ⟶ x + 6 ⟵ Constant

The **Variable** and **Constant** are **Terms** because they are linked by a + **sign**.

A **Coefficient** is a Constant that is associated or connected with a Variable. It stands in front of the Variable. The Value of the Variable is Multiplied by the Coefficient.

Example: | Show a Coefficient attached to a Variable: |

Coefficient ⟶ $2x$ ⟵ Variable

$2x$ is really $2 \times x$.

The **Variable 5** is Multiplied by the **Coefficient** of $\times 2$.

$$2x \longrightarrow 2 \times 5 = 10$$

<u>No Coefficient</u> - treat as if a **1** is present eg. $x = 1x$

An **Expression** is a collection of quantities made up of Constants and Variables linked by Operation signs such as + and −. It <u>usually does not</u> include an Equals Sign.

All Expressions with two or more terms are **Multinomial**. A Multinomial Expression with just two terms is **Binomial**. A Multinomial Expression with three terms is **Trinomial**.

Example: | Show some Multinomial Expressions: |

$$x + y \qquad 3 + x^2 - y \qquad 4(x - y)$$

Binomial   **Trinomial**   **Binomial**

'Like Terms' are those terms that are completely identical in respect to their <u>Variables</u> and <u>Powers</u>. Their Coefficients however can be different.

Example: | Show some 'Like Terms' and 'Unlike Terms': |

'Like Terms' ⟶ $2x$ and x $3y^2$ and $2y^2$

      Same Variables, Coefficients   Same Variables and Powers,
      can be different.   Coefficients can be different.

'Unlike Terms' ⟶ x and y $4y$ and $3y^2$

       Different Variables.   Same Variables but Powers
              must be the same.

An **Algebraic Equation** is a mathematical statement where two Expressions (one can be a Constant) have Equal value.

Example: Show some Equations (two Expressions linked):

Binomial Expression $\longrightarrow$ $2x + 7 = 15$ $\longleftarrow$ Expression (Constant only)

Binomial Expression $\longrightarrow$ $2x + 5 = x + 14 - 4$ $\longleftarrow$ Trinomial Expression

Exercise 20: 12   Answer the following:

Which of these terms:

$$x + 5 - 3y$$

1) are Constants? ....
2) are Variables? ....
3) have Coefficients? ....

4) Is the Expression Binomial or Trinomial? ....

Write whether these terms are 'Like' or 'Unlike':

5) $2x$ and 9 ....   6) $5x$ and $4y$ ....   7) x and $3x$ ....

8) x^2 and $2x$ ....   9) x and y ....   10) $2a^2$ and $4a^2$ ....

6. Algebraic Operations
a. Simplifying Algebraic Expressions

Directed Number rules and BODMAS apply to Algebraic Expressions. To **Simplify** expressions we Add, Subtract, Multiply or Divide the 'Like Terms'.

b. Adding and Subtracting Terms

Expressions are **Simplified** by **Combining** or **Collecting** (Adding or Subtracting) the **'Like Terms'**.

Example: | Add or Subtract Terms with single Variables: |

'Like Terms' can be Added or Subtracted. Note that p means $1p$.

$$3p + p = 4p$$

Example: | Add or Subtract Terms with Multiple Variables: |

Note that xy is the same as yx. The Simplified Expression puts the letters in Alphabetical Order.

$$7xy - 3yx = 4xy$$

Example: | Add and Subtract a number of Terms: |

Collect all the 'Line Terms' (separate y and x Terms and number only Terms).

Add and Subtract the separate Terms.

$$3x + x + 4y - 2x - y + 2y$$
$$= 3x + x - 2x + 4y + 2y - y$$
$$= 2x - 5y$$

Exercise 20: 13   Simplify the following:

1) $7x + 7 - x + 1$

= .... = ...

2) $8y - 3z - 2y + {}^-2z$

= .... = ...

3) $4y - 4z - {}^-2y + 9$

= .... = ...

4) $2a - 4a - b + 8b$

= .... = ...

5) $yz + 2zy - x + 2x$

= .... = ...

6) ${}^-y - 2y + y + z - 5y$

= .... = ...

7) $5xyz + 2xy - 4zyx$

= .... = ...

8) $4c - 3a - 2b + 5a$

= .... = ...

9) ${}^-x + 5x - x + 4y + y$ = ... = ...

10) $y - 3y - 2y + 3z + x$ = ... = ...

19

c. Multiplying and Dividing Terms

Expressions can be **Simplified** by **Multiplying** or **Dividing** 'Like Terms'. The rules are as follows:

Example: Multiply two Variables together:

Leave out the Multiplication sign and place the two Variables next to each other.

$$x \times y = xy$$

Example: Multiply two Variables with Coefficients:

Multiply the Coefficients together and place the Variables next to each other.

$$5x \times 3y = 15xy$$

Example: Multiply two/three Variables that are the same:

Write the Variable and Square it.

$$x \times x = x^2$$

Squared Negative Terms become Positive.

$$-x \times -x = x^2$$

Variables can be Cubed too.

$$x \times x \times x = x^3$$

Example: Multiply two same Variables with Coefficients:

Multiply the two Coefficients together and Square the Variable.

$$3y \times 4y = 12y^2$$

Example: Multiply two same and one different Variable:

Square the same Variables, then Multiply with the different Variable.

$$y \times x \times x = yx^2$$

Example: Divide two Variables:

Write the Variables in the form of a Fraction.

$$x \div y = \frac{x}{y}$$

An Expression Simplifies just like any other Fraction:

$$\frac{2x}{2y} = \frac{x}{y}$$

Exercise 20: 14   Simplify the following:

1) $5x \times -7$
= ....

2) $y \times yx$
= ....

3) $5x \div y =$ ....

20

4) $\dfrac{10y}{5}$ = ...

5) $y \times 7xy$ = ...

6) $y \times y \times y$ = ...

7) $5x \times 5x \times y \div 4$ = ...

8) $24x \div \text{-}6$ = ...

9) $2a \times b \times b$ = ...

10) $2z \times 4x \times 3y$ = ...

d. Brackets and Expansion

All the previous rules for Brackets apply. Any digit or Variable outside a Bracket Multiplies (**Expands**) each term separately inside the Bracket (**Distributive Rule**):

Example: | Expand and Solve $2(a + b)$: |

$$2(a + b) \longrightarrow (2 \times a) + (2 \times b) \longrightarrow 2a + 2b$$

With more complex Expressions expand the Brackets and then collect the 'Like Terms'.

Example: | Expand and Solve $2(x - 1) + (2x + y)$: |

$2(x - 1) + 3(x + y)$

$2x - 2 + 3x + 3y)$

$5x + 3y - 2$

Brackets can represent Squared Numbers. Negative Terms outside a Bracket change all the signs within the Bracket.

Example: | Expand the Expression: $\text{-}x(x + 4y)$ |

$(\text{-}x \times x) + (\text{-}x \times 4y)$

$\text{-}x^2 + \text{-}4xy$

Exercise 20: 15 Multiply out the Brackets:

1) $4(a + 3b)$

= ....

2) $5(x - 3)$

= ....

3) $x(y + z)$

= ....

4) $a(3a - 2b)$ 5) $-a(a - b)$ 6) $2(3a + 4b)$

= .... = ... = ...

Multiply out the **Brackets**, then **Collect 'Like Terms'**

7) $3(a + 2) + 2(a + b)$ 8) $x(-x + 5) + 2(x - y)$

= .... = ...

= .... = ...

9) $4(-x - 5) + 2(x - 3)$ 10) $4(a - b) - 3(a + b)$

= .... = ...

= .... = ...

7. Substitution

Replacing a Variable (letter) with a Number is called **Substitution**. Substitute the given Values for the Letters. Expressions are calculated using the Order of Operations:

Example: If $x = 4$ work out the value of $3(x - 2)$:

$x = 4$ $3(x - 2)$ **Substitute** 4 for x ⟶ $3(4 - 2)$

Multiply Out the brackets as usual ⟶ $12 - 6 = 6$

Exercise 20: 16 Find the value of these Expressions:

If $x = 5$; $y = 3$; $z = 2$

1) $5x + 3y - z$ 2) xyz 3) $x(x + 2) + 2z$

= .... = ... = ...

4) $-3(2y + z) + yz$ 5) $8(x - y) - z$

= .... = ...

22

$$\text{If } a = 6 \quad b = {}^-4 \quad c = 2$$

6) $\dfrac{a + c}{b} = \ \text{........}$

7) $3a - 2b$ $= \ \text{........}$

8) $5(c + b)$ $= \ \text{........}$

9) $3a + c^3 - b$ $= \ \text{........}$

10) $\dfrac{a^2 + b^2 + 8}{c(2 + 4)} = \ \text{........}$

8. More Number Sequences

A **Sequence** is a set of numbers or objects made or written in order, according to a mathematical rule. See (**Book 1**, **pp. 32-33**) for introductory work on Number Sequences.

Each value in the Sequence is called a **Term**. It is Algebra because there are **Missing Terms** (usually denoted by *n*).

a. Using the Gaps

There is an Operational relationship between the numbers. The Four Rules of Number $+ - \times \div$ give the basis for solving all Sequences. Look for what is happening in the gaps between the numbers.

Example: What is the rule for this Number Sequence?

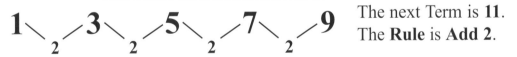

The next Term is **11**.
The **Rule** is **Add 2**.

1. Numbers may **Leapfrog** over each other and create two Sequences. eg. **2, 1, 4, 2, 6, 3, 8, 4** (2, 4, 6, 8) (1, 2, 3, 4)

2. **A Quick Guide to Operations**:

Adding	- Numbers get **bigger slowly**
Multiplying	- Numbers get **bigger quickly**
Subtracting	- Numbers get **smaller slowly**
Dividing	- Numbers get **smaller quickly**

b. Common Number Patterns

Familiarity with certain Sequence types can save time.

Example: | Show the most common types of Sequences: |

Arithmetic Progression - Each new Term is made by Adding a constant amount to the previous Term.

1, 4, 7, 10, 13, 16 Add 3 - Next Term **19**

Geometric Progression - Each new Term is made by Multiplying the previous Term by a constant amount.

1, 4, 16, 64 Times by 4 - Next Term is **256**

Doubling Sequence - Each new Term is twice the value of the previous Term.

1, 2, 4, 8, 16 Times by 2 - Next Term is **32**

Fibonacci Sequence - Each new Term is made by Adding together the previous two Terms starting at | 1, 1 |

| **1, 1,** **2, 3, 5, 8** **Add two previous Terms** Next Term is **13**

Lucas Sequence - Each new Term is made by Adding together the previous two Terms starting at | 1, 3 |

| **1, 3,** **4, 7, 11, 18** **Add two previous Terms** Next Term is **29**

Alternating Sequence - Terms are alternately Positive and Negative **1, -1, 2, -2, 3, -3** Next Term is **4**

Square Numbers (nth Term is n^2) **1, 4, 9, 16, 25**

Cube Numbers (nth Term is n^3) **1, 8, 27, 64, 125**

Triangular Numbers **1, 3, 6, 10, 15, 21**

Rectangular Numbers **6, 8, 10, 12, 14, 15**

Prime Numbers **2, 3, 5, 7, 11, 13, 17**

Exercise 20: 17   Find the Missing Terms:

1) **21, 15, 10, 6,** ......, ...   2) **1, 5, 25, 125,** ......, ...

3) **10, 12, 14, 15,** ......, ...   4) **0, -1, -3, -6,** ......, ...

5) **7, 11, 18, 29,** ......, ...   6) **5, 7, 11, 13,** ......, ...

7) **80, 40, 20, 10,** ......, ...   8) **1, 4, 9, 16,** ......, ...

9) **1, 2, 6, 24, 120,** ....   10) **216, 125, 64,** ......, ...

9. Finding the *nth* Term
a. The Inductive Rule

Arithmetic Progressions follow the **Inductive Rule** (The **Previous Term** is used as a basis for finding the next Term). These Progressions have **Equal Spacing** between Terms.

Example: Find the *nth* Term through the Inductive Rule:

$$4 \diagdown_6 \diagup 10 \diagdown_6 \diagup 16 \diagdown_6 \diagup 22 \diagdown_6 \diagup 28 \quad ....$$

The pattern adds **6** - the next Term is: $\mathbf{28 + 6 = 34}$

The **10th** Term can be worked out by counting forward.

$$\mathbf{28 + 6 + 6 + 6 + 6 + 6 = 58}$$
    5th term + 5 more 6s   **10th term**

It is not practical to count forward to the **100th** Term.

The **100th** Term is **95** Terms more than the **5th** Term:

$$\mathbf{28 + (95 \times 6) = 598}$$

Last Term - 28 + (95 Terms more × gap of 6) = 100th Term - 598

Exercise 20: 18a   Find the *nth* Term by Induction:

1) **6, 11, 16, 21, 26** a) **13**th Term ..... b) **19**th Term .....

2) **3, 10, 17, 24, 31** a) **15**th Term ..... b) **23**th Term .....

b. The Difference Method

The **Difference Method** does not use the previous Term (not Inductive). Only the **Term number** is required (this is the Term we wish to find eg. 14th Term). An Algebraic Rule will apply to all Terms that follow this particular pattern.

Example: | Find the ***nth*** Term by the Difference Method: |

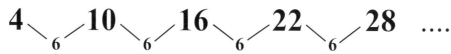

1. What is the **gap** between each number? It is **6**.

2. It is therefore related to the **6 times table**.

3. It is the **6 times table** shifted **2** places to the left for this particular Sequence.

Six Times Table

| 6 | 12 | 18 | 24 | 30 | 36 | 42 |

−2 −2 −2 −2 −2 −2 −2

4   10   16   22   28   34   40

Sequence

The Algebraic Rule

The ***nth*** Number is Multiplied by the gap of **6**.

It is expressed **6n**

The original Number pattern is **2** less than the **6 times table**.

It is expressed as **−2**

The Rule is: $6n - 2$

The **10th** Term will be: $6 \times 10 - 2 = 58$

The **100th** Term will be: $6 \times 100 - 2 = 598$

Exercise 20: 18b Find using the Difference Method:

3) a) **3, 5, 7, 9, 11** Algebraic Rule is ....

 b) What is the **14**th Term? .... **19**th Term? ....

4) a) **3, 7, 11, 15, 19** Algebraic Rule is ....

   b) What is the **15**th Term? .... **32**nd Term? ....

5) a) **6, 11, 16, 21, 26** Algebraic Rule is ....

   b) What is the **12**th Term? .... **16**th Term? ....

c. Using the Formula

An expression for the **nth** Number or Term in a Sequence can be found using the following Formula:

The **nth** Term is usually expressed as U_n (Unknown Number).

The **nth** Term we need to find.

The **first Number** in the Sequence.

$$U_n = dn + (a - d)$$

The **difference** between each pair of Numbers

Example: | Write an Expression for the **nth** Number of this Sequence: **2, 7, 12, 17, 22**

$$U_n = dn + (a - d)$$
$$U_n = 5n + (2 - 5)$$
$$U_n = 5n - 3$$

- The first Number is **2**
- The difference between each pair of Numbers is **5**

This is an Expression for the **nth** Number of this Sequence.

Example: | Find the **15th** Number of the same Sequence: **2, 7, 12, 17, 22**

$$U_{15} = 5n - 3 \longrightarrow U_{15} = 5 \times 15 - 3$$

Substitution

This is **15th** Number of this Sequence.

$$U_{15} = 75 - 3$$
$$U_{15} = 72$$

Exercise 20: 18c Find using the Formula:

6) a) **7, 12, 17, 22, 27** Algebraic Rule U_n = ...

   b) The **18**th Term is? U_{18} = ... **29**th Term? U_{29} = ...

7) a) **5, 11, 17, 23, 29** Algebraic Rule U_n = ...

   b) The **16**th Term is? U_{16} = ... **38**th Term is? U_{38} = ...

Study the match patterns. Write down an Algebraic Rule for the **nth** pattern using **m** for matches. Then find the number of matches required in each case for the pattern:

8) a) Rule is **m** = ... b) **15th** pattern .... matches.

Pattern 1   Pattern 2   Pattern 3

9) a) Rule is **m** = ...

   b) **23rd** pattern

    .... matches.

10) a) Rule is **m** = ... b) **15th** pattern .... matches.

10. Trial and Improvement

Sometimes a missing value (**x**) is found by **Trial** and **Error**. It can be a Whole Number or a Decimal Value. We find it by **Substituting** values into an Equation and testing them out.

Example: | Find the value of **x** in **10 − x = 4**:

$$10 - x = 4 \longrightarrow \text{Try } x = 6 \longrightarrow 10 - 6 = 4$$

Finding the **Missing Value** x can often require repeated Substitutions before the correct value is discovered. Some Equations have x **values** on both sides adding complexity.

Example: | Find the value of x in $2x + 3 = 5 + x$ |

| Try $x = 1$ | $2x + 3 = 5 + x$ | This does not balance as the **right side** is **too big**. |

$$2 + 3 = 5 + 1$$
$$5 = 6$$

| Try $x = 3$ | $2x + 3 = 5 + x$ | This does not balance as the l**eft side** is **too big**. |

$$2 \times 3 + 3 = 5 + 3$$
$$9 = 8$$

| Try $x = 2$ | $2x + 3 = 5 + x$ | This works as **both sides balance**. |

$$2 \times 2 + 3 = 5 + 2$$
$$7 = 7$$

Exercise 20: 19a   Use Trial and Error to find x:

Choose values from the boxes to try out in the Equations.

1) $3x + 5 = 2x + 8$ | 1; 2; 3; 4 | $x = $ ....

2) $5x - 4 = 5 + 2x$ | 1; 2; 3 | $x = $ ....

3) $x - 2 = 3x - 12$ | 2; 3; 4; 5 | $x = $ ....

4) $8 + 4x = 3x + 14$ | 4; 5; 6; 7 | $x = $ ....

5) $9x + 4 = 20 + 5x$ | 1; 2; 3; 4 | $x = $ ....

Finding the **Missing Value** x when it has been **Squared** or **Cubed** involves working with Decimals. A calculator is normally used for such calculations. Easier examples can be done on paper (<u>Long Multiplication</u> is often required).

Example: | Find the value of x in $x^3 + 8 = 30$ |

An x **value** has to be found to make the Equation work $\longrightarrow$

$$x^3 + 8 = 30$$
$$3^3 + 8 =$$
$$(3 \times 3 \times 3) + 8 =$$
$$27 + 8 = 35$$

| Try $x = 3$ |

$x = 3$ is **too big**, so try a Decimal Value <u>below</u> this.

| Try $x = 2.75$ |
$$2.75^3 + 8 =$$
$$(2.75 \times 2.75 \times 2.75) + 8 =$$
$$20.8 + 8 = 28.8$$

$x = 2.75$ is **too small**, so try a Decimal Value <u>above</u> this.

| Try $x = 2.8$ |
$$2.8^3 + 8 =$$
$$(2.8 \times 2.8 \times 2.8) + 8 =$$
$$21.952 \ (\text{Rounds to } 22) + 8 = 30$$

| Therefore $x = 2.8$ |

Exercise 20: 19b

Test the values in the boxes and <u>choose</u> x to 1 d.p.

6) $x^2 = 5$ | Multiply by itself **2** times: | **2.1** **2.3** **2.2** | $x = $ ....

7) $x^3 = 20$ | Multiply by itself **3** times: | **2.6** **2.8** **2.7** | $x = $ ....

8) $x^2 - x = 7$ | This Equation has two Terms. | **2. 9** ^{3} **3. 1** $^{3.\,2}$

Test out each value and Substitute it into the Equation:

e.g. Try $x = 2.9$ $x^2 = 2.9 \times 2.9 = 8.41$

$x^2 - x = 7 \longrightarrow$ Substitute $\longrightarrow 8.41 - 2.9 = 5.51$ (too small)

Now try out the other values to find x: $x = \ \ldots\ldots$

9) $x^2 + x = 5$ | **1. 6** **1. 7** **1. 8** **1. 9** | $x = \ \ldots\ldots$

10) $5x - x^2 = 5$ | **3. 4** **3. 5** **3. 6** **3. 7** | $x = \ \ldots\ldots$

11. Algebraic Equations
a. Linear Equations

A **Linear Equation** is an Equation that only has **First Order Terms**. This means Squared or Cubed terms are not used. It is solved by finding the value of the missing number or Variable (First Order Term). They can be written as Arithmetic Equations, Function Machines or as Algebraic Equations.

Example: | Show how a Linear Equation can be written:

$\boxed{?} - 6 = 13$ $? \rightarrow \boxed{-6} \rightarrow 13$ $x - 6 = 13$

Arithmetic Equation   Function Machine   Algebraic Equation

Linear Equations in an Algebraic form replace the missing amount with a Variable (letter) such as x or y.

Algebraic Linear Equations can be solved in three ways:
1) **Reverse Function Machines**.
2) **Reverse Operations**.
3) **Balancing** (Doing the same thing to both sides).

b. Reverse Function Machines

Reverse Function Machines can be used Algebraically:

Example: Solve $3x - 4 = 17$ with a Function Machine:

The **Variable** x can be fed into a Function Machine to produce the Equation.

IN	OPERATION	OUT
$x \rightarrow$	$\boxed{\times 3} \xrightarrow{3x} \boxed{-4} \rightarrow$	$3x - 4$

The **Constant** 17 is now fed into the Reverse Machine to give the value of x.

$\longleftarrow$ **Go backwards**

$7 \leftarrow \boxed{\div 3} \xleftarrow{21} \boxed{+4} \leftarrow 17$

$x = 7$ satisfies the Equation $3x - 4 = 17$

Exercise 20: 20a   Solve the shaded Equations:

1) $3y + 1 = 10$ $y \rightarrow \boxed{\times 3} \xrightarrow{3y} \boxed{+1} \rightarrow 3y + 1$

...... $\leftarrow \boxed{\div 3} \xleftarrow{9} \boxed{-1} \leftarrow 10$ The **Constant** 10 is fed into the **Reverse Machine**.

- -

2) $\dfrac{a - 2}{4} = 7$ $a \rightarrow \boxed{-2} \xrightarrow{a-2} \boxed{\div 4} \rightarrow \dfrac{a - 2}{4}$

...... $\leftarrow \boxed{+2} \xleftarrow{28} \boxed{\times 4} \leftarrow 7$ The **Constant** 7 is fed into the **Reverse Machine**.

- -

3) $4b - 5 = 3$ ...... $\leftarrow \boxed{\div 4} \xleftarrow{8} \boxed{+5} \leftarrow 3$

4) $3a + 3 = 18$ ...... $\leftarrow \boxed{} \leftarrow \boxed{} \leftarrow 18$

5) $\dfrac{x}{4} - 10 = 6$ ...... $\leftarrow \boxed{} \leftarrow \boxed{} \leftarrow 6$

32

c. Reverse Operations

Reverse Operations can solve Algebraic Equations:

Example: Solve $\frac{x}{8} + 6 = 14$ with Reverse Operations:

The objective is to get x on its own on one side of the Equation. When a term is moved to the other side its sign changes. Inverse Operations apply:

Add ⟷ Subtract

Multiply ⟷ Divide

To keep the values Positive move the smaller Constants to the opposite side first.

$\frac{x}{8} + 6 = 14$ Turn the + 6 to − 6 by changing sides.

$\frac{x}{8} = 14\,(-6)$

$\frac{x}{8} = 8$ Turn the ÷ 8 to ×8 by changing sides.

$x = 8\,(\times 8)$

$x = 64$

Exercise 20: 20b   Solve these Equations:

6) $\frac{x}{4} - 7 = 1$

$x = \ldots\ldots$

7) $6x + 4 = 28$

$x = \ldots\ldots$

8) $18 = 3a + 3$

This Equation is round the other way. Collect a on the right instead of the left, then do it in the same way.

$a = \ldots\ldots$

9) $1 = 4y - 15$

$y = \ldots\ldots$

10) $8x + 2 = 18$

$x = \ldots\ldots$

d. Balancing

The **Balancing Method** requires the unknown value to be moved to one side of the Equation and numbers to the other side. The = sign acts like a weighing scale. <u>Whatever action is carried out on one side must be done to the other side.</u>

Example: | Find the value of x if $3x + 6 = 24$: |

Equations require Adding and Subtracting to be done before Multiplying and Dividing.

$$3x + 6 = 24$$

1. Deal with Add/Subtract first. Subtract **6** to Cancel the **+ 6**.

Subtract 6 from both sides
$$3x + \cancel{6} = 24 \quad {}^{-6}_{\ -6}$$

2. Subract **6** from **24** on the other side.

$$3x = 24 - 6$$

Divide both sides by 3

3. **3x** is really **3 × x**. To get x alone we Divide **3x** by **3**.

$$\frac{\cancel{3}x}{\cancel{3}} = 18^{\div 3}$$

4. Divide **18** by **3** to find the value of x.

$$x = \frac{18}{3}$$

5. x is now on its own.

$$x = 6$$

Exercise 20: 21a   Solve these Equations:

1) $3x - 4 = 17$

$x = $ ....

2) $3x + 9 = 36$

$x = $ ....

3) $\dfrac{x}{18} + 3 = 6$

$x = $ ....

4) $3y - 9 = 27$

$y = $ ....

e. Equations with Variables on Both Sides

Equations with more than one Variable either side can be solved in a similar way. The rule is 'Get rid of the smallest letter term by moving it to the other side of the Equals Sign'.

Example: Find the value of $4x - 28 = 3x + 4$

If an Equation has two same type Variables these must be Combined first.

Two Variables

$$4x - 28 = 3x + 4$$

1. Cancel **3x** by Subtracting.

$$4x - 28 = \cancel{3x}^{-3x} + 4$$

2. Balance by placing **-3x** from the other side.

$$4x - 3x - 28 = 4$$

3. Subtract the two letter terms **4x – 3x** to give *x*.

$$x - 28 = 4$$

4. Cancel **-28** by Adding **28** to the same side.

$$x - \cancel{28}^{+28} = 4$$

5. Balance it by Adding **28** to the other side.

$$x = 4 + 28$$

6. Add **4** and **28** to find *x*.

$$x = 32$$

Exercise 20: 21b   Solve these Equations:

5) $2y + 3 = 13 - 3y$ 6) $9 + x = 17 - 3x$

$y = \text{.......}$ $x = \text{.......}$

7) $2x + 2 = 5x - 4$ 8) $4x - 1 = 17 - 2x$

$x = \text{........}$ $x = \text{........}$

f. Checking Equations by Substitution

Once an Equation has been solved it can be checked by Substitution. Example:

Check the Solution to $3x + 2 = 2x + 9$ by Substitution:

1. The Solution to this Equation is **7**.

2. Substitute **7** into the Equation.

3. The Equation balances.

$$3x + 2 = 2x + 9$$

$$x = 7$$

$$(3 \times 7) + 2 = (2 \times 7) + 9$$

$$23 = 23$$

Exercise 20: 21c Solve these Equations:

9) a) $6a - 3 = 2a + 13$ 10) a) $2x - 5 = 5x - 11$

$a = \text{........}$ $x = \text{........}$

Substitute into the Equations to check they work:

9) b) $6a - 3 = 2a + 13$ 10) b) $2x - 5 = 5x - 11$

$\text{......} = \text{......}$ $\text{......} = \text{......}$

It Balances? - Yes or no?........   It Balances? - Yes or no?........

12. Algebraic Formulae
a. What is a Formula?

A Formula is a **Mathematical Rule**, usually written as an Equation. If a number is Substituted into the Formula it will be changed into another number by Mathematical Operations. Many **Arithmetic formulae** have been used in **Books 1-5**.

Example: | Give the Formula for the Area of a Rectangle: |

Area = **Length** × **Width** (This is true for all Rectangles).

Algebraic Formulae are Equations that also state a rule that can either be applied generally or just to a particular question. They use **Symbols** or **Letters** to denote the missing Variable. Many Formulae can be stated in an Algebraic form:

Example: | Write a Formula for the Perimeter of a Square: |

P = 4L (Perimeter = 4 × Length of one Side - True for all Squares).

b. Temperature Formulae

Degrees Fahrenheit (^{o}F) is the old fashioned Temperature Scale and **Degrees Celsius** (^{o}C) is the modern Temperature Scale. Approximate conversions are shown on this table:

Standard Temperatures	Freezing Point	Room Temp	A Very Hot Day	Body Temp	Boiling Point
Celsius	0^oC	20^oC	30^oC	37.4^oC	100^oC
Fahrenheit	32^oF	68^oF	86^oF	99.3^oF	212^oF

Celsius is calibrated using the freezing and boiling point of water.

Algebraic Formulae are used for difficult conversions from Fahrenheit to Celsius and vice versa.

a. Fahrenheit to Celsius
Substitute Fahrenheit into this Formula to find Celsius.

$$C = \frac{5}{9}(F - 32)$$

37

Example: | Convert **43**$^{\circ}$ Fahrenheit to Celsius:

$$C = \frac{5}{9}(F - 32)$$

$$C = \frac{5}{9}(43 - 32)$$

$$C = \frac{5}{9}(11)$$

$$C = (5 \div 9) \times 11$$

$$C = 0.56 \times 11$$

$$C = 6.16 \text{ (Rounds to 6)}.$$

$$\boxed{43^{\circ}F = 6^{\circ}C}$$

Exercise 20: 22a Convert Temperatures from $^{\circ}F$ to $^{\circ}C$
(Round to whole Degrees).

1) **67**$^{\circ}$**F** = ...$^{\circ}$C

2) **39**$^{\circ}$**F** = ...$^{\circ}$C   4) **12**$^{\circ}$**F** = ...$^{\circ}$C

3) **59**$^{\circ}$**F** = ...$^{\circ}$C   5) **80**$^{\circ}$**F** = ...$^{\circ}$C

---

b. Celsius to Fahrenheit
Substitute Fahrenheit into this Formula to find Celsius.

$$F = \frac{9}{5}C + 32$$

Example: | Convert **5**$^{\circ}$ Celsius to Fahrenheit:

$$F = \frac{9}{5}C + 32$$

$$F = \frac{9}{5}5 + 32$$

$$F = (9 \div 5) \times 5 + 32$$

$$F = (1.8 \times 5) + 32$$

$$F = 9 + 32$$

$$F = 41$$

$$\boxed{5^{\circ}C = 41^{\circ}F}$$

Exercise 20: 22b Convert Temperatures from $^{\circ}C$ to $^{\circ}F$
(Round to whole Degrees).

6) **21**$^{\circ}$**C** = ...$^{\circ}$F

7) **16**$^{\circ}$**C** = ...$^{\circ}$F   9) **-10**$^{\circ}$**C** = ...$^{\circ}$F

8) **2**$^{\circ}$**C** = ...$^{\circ}$F   10) **27**$^{\circ}$**C** = ...$^{\circ}$F

c. Turning Words into Formulae

> Statements or Expressions can be converted into Formulae. The Four Rules of Number $+ - \times \div$ provide the basis.

The most common statements for creating Formulae from the Four Rules of Number are listed below:

Addition

more than;   **on top of**;
increased by;   **enlarge**;
added to;   **plus**

Example:

What is **8 <u>more than</u> n**?

$$n + 8 \quad \text{or} \quad 8 + n$$

This can be written in two ways because Addition is Commutative (See **p. 3**).

Subtraction

is taken away;   **from**;
decreased by; **reduced**;
is removed;   **less than**

Example:

What is **8 <u>less than</u> n**?

$$n - 8$$

This cannot be written as $8 - n$ as because Subtraction is **not** Commutative (See **p. 3**).

Multiplication

increased by a factor of;
tripled;   **doubled**;
lots of;   **quadrupled**

Example:

What is **8 <u>lots of</u> n**?

$$n8 \quad \text{or} \quad 8n$$

This can be written in two ways since Multiplication is Commutative (See **p. 3**).

Division

reduced by a factor of;
shared out; **Divided up**;
halved;   **split between**

Example:

What is **8 <u>shared out between</u> n**?	$\longrightarrow \dfrac{8}{n}$

This cannot be written as $\dfrac{n}{8}$ because Division is **not** Commutative (See **p. 3**).

Exercise 20: 23   Write as Formulae:

1) **7** more than **n** ....
2) **b** split between **8** ....
3) Twice **y** plus **x** ....
4) **c** decreased by **7** ....
5) **3** less than **4** lots of **x** ....
6) **5** less than **y** ....
7) **5** plus **n**, shared between **y** ....
8) Triple **n** take away **6**, reduced by a factor of **4** ....
9) **x** increased by **5** then divided up by **y** ....
10) **p** halved minus **r** ....

d. Formulaic Expressions

Formulae can be used to represent and solve problems:
Look out for the Four Rules of Number $+ - \times \div$.

Example: Write this sentence as an Algebraic Expression:

A prize of **x** pounds is shared among **4** children. How many pounds does each child receive?

Each child receives $\dfrac{x}{4}$ pounds or $\dfrac{1}{4}x$ pounds.

Exercise 20: 24a   Write as Algebraic Expressions:

1) A piece of cloth measures **y** metres and is cut into **5** equal lengths. Each piece measures .... metres.

2) Tom trains for a cross country race. He runs **x** miles every day after school and twice as far on Saturday and Sunday. How many miles does he run in one week? .... miles.

3) **50** children are taken on a school trip. Each child takes £**x** for the fare and £**y** for pocket money. What is the total amount taken by the group? .... pounds.

4) Mary scored *m* marks in Maths, *e* marks in English and *s* marks in Science. Mary's Average mark was ....

5) Nikhil earns *x* pounds **each week** from his paper round. He also gets *y* pounds **each month** from his parents. How much does Nikhil get in one year? .... pounds.

e. Formulaic Equations

Sentences can be written as Equations if their wording requires an **Equals Sign**. Example:

is; total; is the same as; gives the same answer as; find; find the answer to

Cooking instructions for the Christmas turkey: Allow **20** mins cooking time for each pound plus an extra **45** mins.

Write a formula for the **Total** time taken *(T)* to cook the turkey where *w* represents the weight of the turkey in lbs.

The Equation can be expressed as: $T = 20w + 45$

If amounts are supplied the Equation offers a Solution:

$T = 20w + 45$
$T = 20 \times 15 + 45$
$T = 345$ **mins** or **5 hrs 45 mins**

How long would it take to cook a **15lb** turkey?

Exercise 20: 24b Write and Solve as Equations:

6) If *x* sweets cost **50p**, write down a Formula for the cost *C* in pence of one sweet and then solve the problem below:

   a) *C* = ... b) What is the cost of **30** sweets? ....

7) To find *y*, Square *x*, Divide this by **2** and Add **3**.

   a) Equation: *y* = ... b) If *x* is **4** find *y* ....

8) There are **27** children in a class and they divide themselves into <u>two equal teams</u> for games. There are **9** who arrive too late to play. (Clue - Use **2x** for teams).
   a) The Equation is ....
   b) How many children in each team? .... children.

Questions are more complex if the Equation has to be created from **two Binomial Expressions**:

Example: | Write this sentence as an Algebraic Equation: |

| Paula found that if she Multiplied the number of sweets (*x*) she had by **5** and Subtracted **2** it was **the same as** if she Added **18** to the number of sweets. |

If the number of sweets was *x*, Multiplying by 5 and Subtracting 2 would give the Expression: $5x - 2$

Adding **18** to the number of sweets (*x*) gives: $x + 18$

Equating these Expressions gives: $5x - 2 = x + 18$

This can now be solved:
$$5x - 2 = x + 18$$
$$5x = x + 20$$
$$4x = 20$$

$$x = 5 \text{ sweets}$$

Exercise 20: 24c Find and Solve the Equation:

9) Ben worked out that if he took his age (*x*), Multiplied it by **2** and Added **4**, it would give the same answer as Adding **14** to his age.

   a) Equation .... = ... b) Solution *x* = ...

----

10) Andy counted his savings. He found that if he took the amount of money he had (*y*), Multiplied it by **4** and then Subtracted **9** he would get the same amount as if he counted the money he had and Added **15** pounds.

   a) Equation .... = ... b) Solution *y* = ...

f. Formulae and Diagrams

Drawing diagrams can help you understand some questions:

Examples: | Express sentences as an Algebraic Formula: |

| Hamza will be x years old **8** years from now. How old was he **8** years ago? |

1. Start from **NOW**.
2. x is **8** years from now

$$\text{Now} \xrightarrow{\ +8\ } x$$

3. Count back from now **8** years to find out how old Hamza was **8** years ago.

$$x-16 \xleftarrow{\ -8\ } \text{Now} \xrightarrow{\ +8\ } x$$

Hamza was $x-16$ years eight years ago.

| John and Priya plant some tomato seeds on the same day. After **1** week both seedlings are **7** cm tall. During the next three weeks John's seedling grows y cm per week and Priya's grows x cm per week. Priya's plant is taller. When the seedlings are four weeks old how much taller is Priya's seedling than John's in cm? |

1. Both seedlings are the same height after the first week so this can be ignored.
2. Priya's seedling grows taller.
3. The difference between Priya's and John's seedlings is:

$3(x-y)$ Priya's Seedling is this much taller.

Priya (x) John (y)

3 weeks is $3x$ She is taller by $3(x-y)$

3 weeks is $3y$

1st week   7cm

Exercise 20: 25a Answer the following:

1) In **3** years time Charlotte's dog will be x years old. How old was her dog **8** years ago? ....

2) A batsman is bowled out after scoring *r* runs. If he had scored **10** more runs he would have twice as many as the batsman before him who scored **20**. Write an Equation with *r* to show how many runs he scored and then solve it.

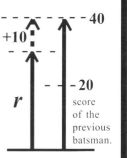

a) Equation .... b) Solution *r* = ...

3) If you multiply a number (*x*) by **3**. Then double it and divide by **6**, the result is **5**. Find the value of *x*.

Solve with Inverse Operations - Reverse Function Machine.

x = ... ← ☐ ─ ☐ ─ ☐ ← **5**

g. Formulae and Shapes

Perimeter and Area of Shapes can be given as a Formula:

Examples: | Write a Formula for the Area of this Octagon: |

1. Notice that the Octagon breaks into Triangles if the Diagonals are drawn in.

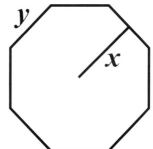

2. The Area Formula for each Triangle is:

Area = $\frac{1}{2}$ base × height

3. Algebraically the Formula is:

Area = $\frac{1}{2}yx$

4. Multiply by **8** for the Area of the Octagon:

Area = $8 × \frac{1}{2}yx$

Area of the Octagon = 4*yx*

Exercise 20: 25b Write as Formulae:

4) Write the Perimeter of this shape as an Algebraic Expression. (Don't forget to Simplify).

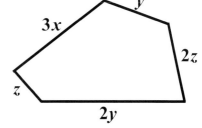

....

5) One side of this Square is **n** cm. Write the Area and Perimeter as Formulae:

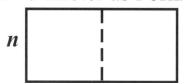

a) Area = ...

b) Perimeter = ...

6) What is the Perimeter of this shape as a Formula:

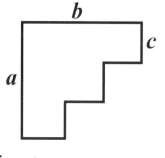

Perimeter = ...

h. Trial and Substitution with Formulae

It may be necessary to Trial and Substitute into a given Formula to find the missing Variable:

Example: | A year 5 class made some Formula cards. Which two of the cards have the same value?

Alice	Bobby	Carol	David
$6x - 6$	$2x + 4$	$8x - 10$	$x + 8$

If we tested **3**, **4** or **5** as **x** they would not work. Only if we substitute **2** into each Formula can we find the right cards.

$6x - 6 = 6 \times 2 - 6 = 6$ $8x - 10 = 8 \times 2 - 10 = 6$

$2x + 4 = 2 \times 2 + 4 = 8$ $x + 8 = 2 + 8 = 10$

Exercise 20: 25c
Some questions require Substitution only and some Trial and Substitution:

7) A boy hires a bicycle for the day whilst on holiday. He is charged **£12** for the first **5** hours, then an hourly rate of **£1. 60** for each additional hour (**h**). Write down a formula (in pence) for the cost of hiring the bicycle. What would it cost to hire the bicycle for **11** hours?

a) $C =$ .... b) **11** hours would cost £ ....

8) A teacher has **6** bags of sweets and **3** loose sweets. Each bag has **s** sweets in it. a) Which Expression shows how many sweets there are altogether? ....

$6s - 4$ $6s + 3$ b) If there are **105** sweets altogether, what is the

$s + 6$ $3 + s$ value of **s** ....

9) Some cards have these expressions written on them:

$4x + 16$ $8x + 4$ $10x + 4$ $4x + 4$

a) Which card has the same value as: $4(x + 4)$ ....

b) By Trial and Substitution find the value of **x** and which two Expressions will make the Equation.

x = ... Equation is .... = ...

10) During a two day fair a school sells choc ices and tubs of ice cream. A choc ice costs **50p** and an ice cream tub costs **40p**. The income **I** is found using the Equation:

$I = 50x + 40y$ **x** is the number of choc ices sold.
y is the number ice cream tubs sold.

a) **Day 1** **x** = **20** and **y** = **35**, so what is **I**? £ ....

b) **Day 2** **I** = **2000** and **x** = **16**, so what is **y**? ....

13. Graphs and Lines

a. Points on a Line

Lines are drawn from Plotting **x** and **y** Coordinates (See **Book 5, pp. 33-34**). A minimum of **2** Coordinates is required but **3** are usually Plotted to ensure accuracy.

Example:

Plot Coordinates and draw the Line of (**1, 2**); (**0, 0**); (**-1, -2**)

Table of Values

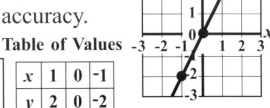

x	1	0	-1
y	2	0	-2

Exercise 20: 26a

Answer the following:

1) Plot the Coordinates and Draw **Line A** from the Table of Values:

x	-2	0	3
y	3	1	-2

2) Fill in the Table of Values from the Plotted Coordinates of **Line B**:

x			
y			

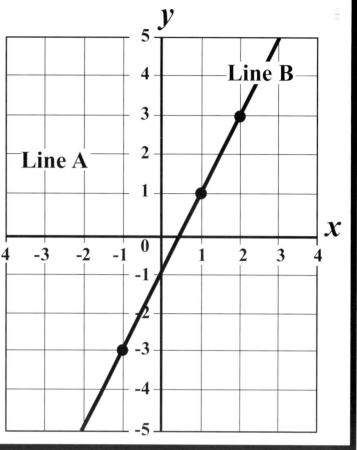

b. Horizontal, Vertical and Diagonal Lines

A **Horizontal Line** Parallel to the **x-axis** is known as $y = a$.

A **Vertical Line** Parallel to the **y-axis** is known as $x = a$.

Example: | Draw lines $y = 3$ and $x = 6$:

The **y**-coordinates for all three points is **3**.

$y = 3$

x	4	2	-3
y	3	3	3

The **x**-axis is the line: $y = 0$.

The **x**-coordinates for all three points is **6**.

$x = 6$

x	-6	-6	-6
y	4	1	-2

The **y**-axis is the line: $x = 0$.

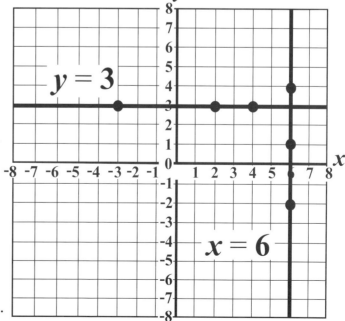

47

A **45°Diagonal Line** bottom left to top right is denoted $y = x$.

A **45°Diagonal Line** bottom right to top left is denoted $y = -x$.

Example: | Draw lines $y = x$ and $y = -x$. |

Both $y = x$ and $y = -x$ go through the Origin (**0, 0**).

y and x Coordinates are Equal at every point.

$y = x$

x	-6	2	6
y	-6	2	6

y and x Coordinates are Equally Opposite at every point.

$y = -x$

x	-3	1	4
y	3	-1	-4

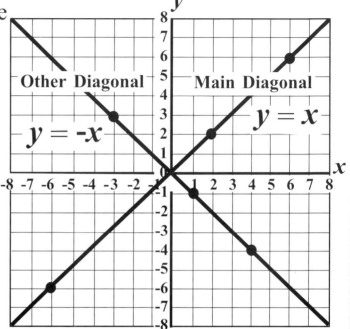

Exercise 20: 26b Identify the following Lines:

3)

$y = $ ....

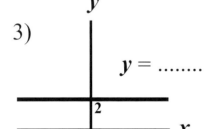

4)

$y = $ ....

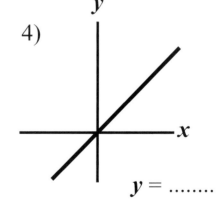

5)

$x = $ ....

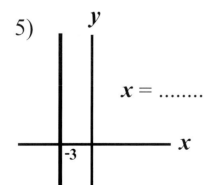

6)

$y = $ ....

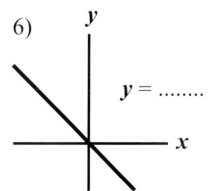

14. Representing Linear Equations

A Linear Equation can be Expressed in **Four** different ways:

Example: Show the ways $y = 2x + 1$ can be Expressed.

1. **Function Machines** - Once the Equation is fed into the Machine it passes through two stages:

$$\text{Stage 1} \qquad \text{Stage 2}$$
$$x \rightarrow \boxed{\times 2} \rightarrow 2x \rightarrow \boxed{+1} \rightarrow 2x + 1$$

$$1.\ y = 2x \quad 2.\ y = x + 1 \rightarrow y = 2x + 1$$

2. **Table of Values** - *x*-values can be given, but if not, you must choose them. Choose sensible values like:

(**-2**, **-1**, **0**, **1** and **2**) *x* is between **-2** and **2**. This can be written:

$-2 \leqslant x \leqslant 2$ *x* is more than or Equal to **-2**; *x* is less than or Equal to **2**.

Each *x*-**value** is **Substituted** into the Number Machine or Equation to create a Table of Values:

x	-2	-1	0	1	2
y	-3	-1	1	3	5

Substituting into the Equation is the standard method.

$$y = 2x + 1$$
$$y = (2 \times \text{-}2) + 1$$
$$y = \text{-}4 + 1$$
$$y = \text{-}3$$

3. **Mappings** - If an Equation is fed into a Mapping it passes through two stages just as it does in a Function Machine:

$$1.\ y = 2x \quad 2.\ y = x + 1 \rightarrow y = 2x + 1$$

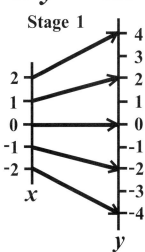
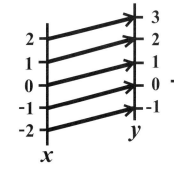
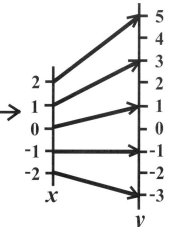

The first two diagrams break the rule down into two parts.
The third Mapping does the rule in one step.

4. **Graphs** - Linear Equations can be shown on a Line Graph.
   To draw a line from an Equation
   a Table of Values has to be created:

   Choose **3** values for *x* and **Substitute** into the Equation:

   $y = 2x + 1$
   $y = (2 \times \text{-}2) + 1$
   $y = 5$

x	-2	0	2
y	-3	1	5

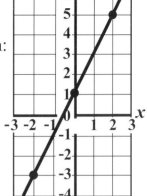

   The *x* and *y* Coordinates are
   plotted from the Table of Values.

All Linear Equations when Plotted will form a **Straight Line**.

15. Mappings

A 'Mapping' represents a
mathematical rule or Equation.
Example:

| Make up a Table of Values and |
| draw a Mapping for $y = 2x$ |

| If *x* = -2 |
| $y = 2x$ |
| $y = 2 \times \text{-}2$ |
| $y = \text{-}4$ |

x	-2	-1	0	1	2
y	-4	-2	0	2	4

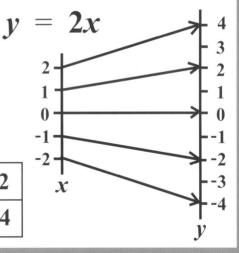

$y = 2x$

Exercise 20: 26c   Answer the following:

7) Draw in the Mapping for: $y = 3x$ (Clue: Think of it as
times by 3. **You do not
need a Table of Values**
for this Mapping).

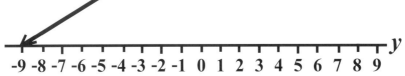

8) <u>Complete the Table of Values</u> and
<u>Draw the Mapping</u> for: $y = x - 3$

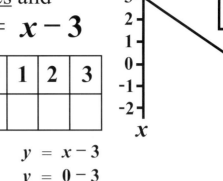

Substitute into
the Equation
to find values:

x	-2	-1	0	1	2	3
y	-5					

$y = x - 3$ $y = x - 3$ $y = x - 3$
$y = -2 - 3$ $y = -1 - 3$ $y = 0 - 3$
$y = -5$ $y = -4$ $y = -3$

---

9) <u>Complete the Table</u> and <u>Draw the Mapping</u> for: $y = x^2$

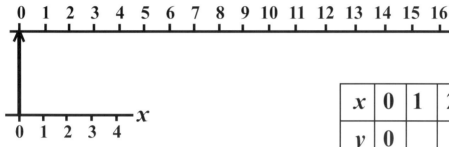

x	0	1	2	3	4
y	0				

This involves finding the **Square**.

---

10) <u>Complete the Table of Values</u>
and Draw the Mapping for:

$y = 3x - 1$

x	-2	-1	0	1	2
y	-7				

Don't forget to **Substitute**
to find the values for the table

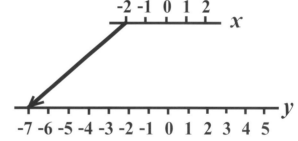

<u>16. Graphs and Linear Equations</u>

Every Linear Equation in two Variables can be written in
the form:

$$y = mx + c$$

m is the **Gradient** (steepness) of the line or
the *x*-coefficient on the *x*-axis. If *m* has a
minus value the Gradient is Negative.

c is the **Gradient
Intercept** on the *y*-axis.

Example: Show that $y = 2x + 1$ demonstrates the pattern for all Linear Equations:

$$y = 2x + 1$$

The **Gradient** of the Line is **2**.

The **Gradient Intercept** on the *y*-axis is **1**.

There are three ways to Draw Linear Graphs:

a. The **Plot the Points** Method (**pp.52-53**).

b. The **Cover and Draw** Method (**pp.54-55**).

c. The **Gradient Intercept** Method (**pp.55-58**).

a. Plot the Points Method

You only need two points to draw a straight line, but it is always best to use three just in case a mistake is made:

Example: Draw lines $y = \frac{x}{3} - 2$ and $y = x + 4$

1. Create a Table of Values for each Linear Equation by choosing three *x*-values and Substituting into each Equation.

2. Plot each point on the *x* and *y* axes and join up the dots.

$y = \dfrac{x}{3} - 2$

x	-3	0	3
y	-3	-2	-1

$y = \dfrac{x}{3} - 2$

$y = \dfrac{-3}{3} - 2$

$y = -1 - 2$

$y = -3$

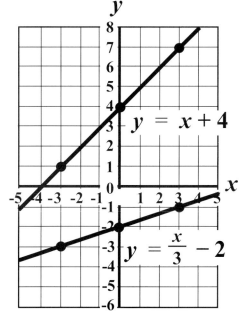

$y = x + 4$

x	-3	0	3
y	1	4	7

$y = x + 4$

$y = -3 + 4$

$y = 1$

Exercise 20: 27a   Answer the following:

1) a) Complete the Table of Values and Draw the Line for the Equation:

$$y = 3x - 2$$

x	0	1	2
y	-2		

b) Does the Line have a Positive or Negative Gradient? ....

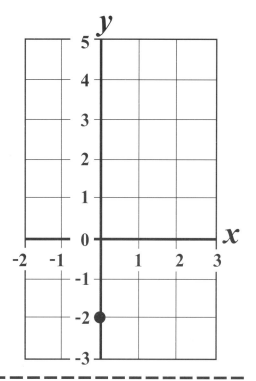

---

2) a) Using the Mapping below choose three **x** and **y Values**, then fill out the Table of Values and Draw the Graph:

$$y = \frac{x}{2} - 1$$

$$y = \frac{x}{2} - 1$$

$$y = \frac{-4}{2} - 1$$

$$y = -2 - 1$$

$$y = -3$$

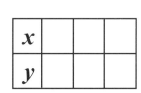

x			
y			

b) Does this Line have a Negative or Positive Gradient?

....

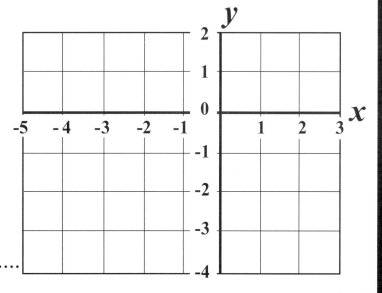

b. Cover and Draw Method

If an equation is written in this form it can be solved simply by the Cover Up Rule:

$$ax + by = c$$

Example: Draw the Graph of $2x + 3y = 15$ using the Cover and Draw Method:

To find the x Coordinate:

Ignore the $3y$ (set $y = 0$).

$2x + \boxed{3y} = 12$

$2x = 12$

$\boxed{x = 6}$

Where the line crosses the x-axis ($x = 6$; $y = 0$).

To find the y Coordinate:

Ignore the $2x$ (set $x = 0$).

$\boxed{2x} + 3y = 12$

$3y = 12$

$\boxed{y = 4}$

Where the line crosses the y-axis ($x = 0$; $y = 4$).

This method only gives 2 Coordinates.

The line crosses the x-axis at **6** and the y-axis at **4**. Plot these points and join them up to form the line.

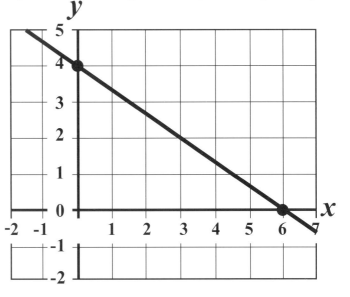

Why it works: When the line crosses the y-axis the x-value is zero and when the line crosses the x-axis the y-value is zero. This means that both the y-value and x-value can be calculated by simply ignoring other values.

Exercise 20: 27b Answer the following:

3) a) Plot and Draw the following Graph:

$$3x - 5y = 15$$

b) Is the Gradient Negative or Positive?

....

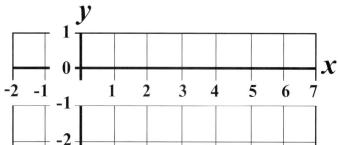

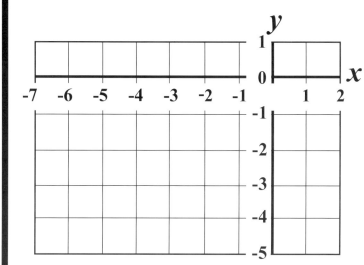

4) a) Plot and Draw the following Graph:

$$2x + 5y = \text{-}10$$

b) Is the Gradient Negative or Positive?

....

c. Gradient Intercept Method

A Line can be drawn from a Linear Equation by using **two pieces of information** contained in the Equation:

Example: | Draw the Graph of $y = 2x + 1$ using the Gradient Intercept Method:

$$y = 2x + 1$$

1. **Gradient of the Line is 2**
(Steepness of the Line).

2. **Gradient Intercept is 1**
(the point where the line cuts the y-axis).

We know that the Line will cross the **y-axis** at **+1** and this is the **Gradient Intercept Point**.

The **Gradient** is **2** and this gives the steepness of the Line.

The Whole Number **2** can be written as a Fraction: $\frac{2}{1}$

Algebraically the **Gradient Formula** expresses it as:

$$\textbf{Gradient} = \frac{\textit{y}\text{-step}}{\textit{x}\text{-step}} = \frac{2}{1} = 2$$

This means for every **y-step** of **2** there is a **x-step** of **1**.

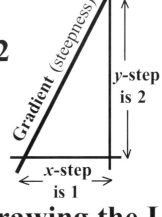

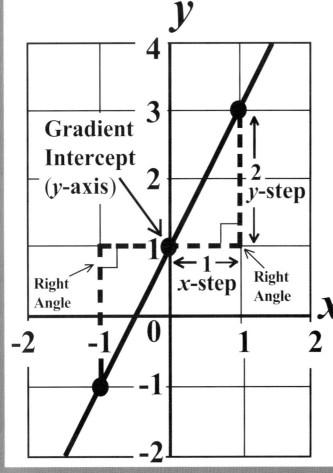

Drawing the Line

1. **x-step** - Draw a Horizontal Line of **1-step** out from either side of the Gradient Intercept Point.

2. Draw a **Right Angle**

3. **y-step** - Draw a Vertical Line of **2-steps** up and down from the Right Angle.

4. **Extend the Line** in either direction.

Gradient defines the relationship between **x** and **y**. (How many **y** per **x**?). Gradient of a Line can be used for various calculations eg. Ratio as a Gradient (See **Book 3 pp. 49-52**). Travel and Conversion Graphs (see **Book 5, pp. 46-47**).

What happens if the Gradient is a **Fraction** and **Negative**?

Example: Draw the line of the Gradient of: $-\dfrac{1}{3}$

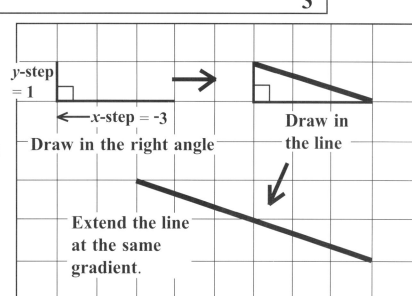

$\dfrac{1 = y\text{-step}}{3 = x\text{-step}}$

When this line is drawn it gives a **Shallow Negative Gradient**:

y-step = 1

← *x*-step = -3

Draw in the right angle

Draw in the line

Extend the line at the same gradient.

Exercise 20: 27c

Answer the following:

5) a) Plot and Draw the following Graph:

$$y = \text{-}2x$$

1. The **Gradient Intercept Point** in this Equation is **0**.

2. The **Gradient** is **-2**.

$$\frac{y\text{-step}}{x\text{-step}} = \frac{2}{1} \quad \text{The minus sign indicates Gradient}$$

b) Does this Graph have a Negative or Positive Gradient? ....

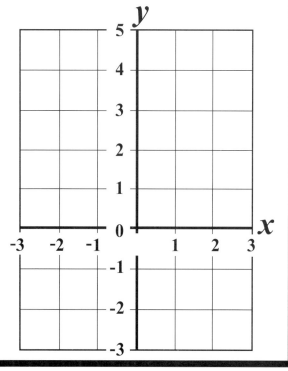

6) a) Plot and Draw the following Graph:

$$y = \frac{x}{2} + 2$$

1. The **Gradient Intercept Point** is **2**

2. The **Gradient** is $\dfrac{x}{2}$

Give x a value. Substitute a **1**

$\dfrac{\textbf{y-step}}{\textbf{x-step}} = \dfrac{\textbf{1}}{\textbf{2}}$ Now calculate the Gradient.

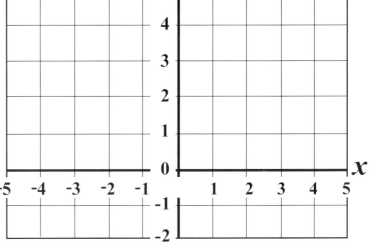

b) Is the Gradient Positive or Negative? ....

17. Bucket Graphs

Bucket shaped or curved Graphs have Equations with x^2 in them. They are often in the form:

$$y = x^2 + a$$

Substitute values for x^2 to give y.

a is the **Point of Intercept** on the y-axis.

Example: | Draw the Bucket Graph for: $y = x^2 - 2$

1. Make a Table of Values using **-3** to **3**. (Choose a set of values - include Negative and Positive values in the table):

Substitute x values into the Equation to find y values:

$y = x^2 - 2$

$y = -3^2 - 2$

$y = (-3 \times -3) - 2$

$y = 9 - 2$

$y = 7$

2. Plot points and Draw Graph.

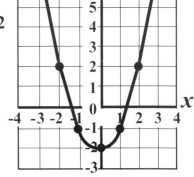

x	-3	-2	-1	0	1	2	3
y	7	2	-1	-2	-1	2	7

Exercise 20: 27d

Answer the following:

7) Complete the Table of Values and Draw the Graph for:

$$y = x^2 + 1$$

x	-3	-2	-1	0	1	2	3
y	10						

Substitute x values into the Equation to find the y values.

$$y = x^2 + 1$$
$$y = -3^2 + 1$$
$$y = (-3 \times -3) + 1$$
$$y = 9 + 1$$
$$y = 10$$

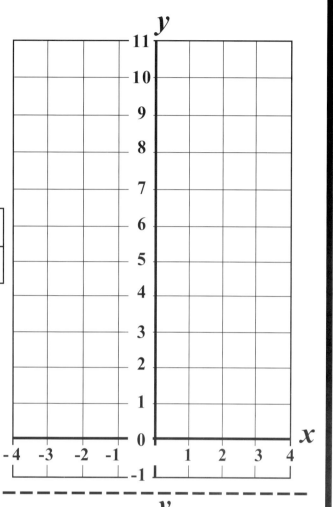

8) Complete the Table of Values and Draw the Graph for:

$$y = x^2$$

x	-3						
y	9						

Substitute x values into the Equation to find the y values.

$$y = -3^2$$
$$y = (-3 \times -3)$$
$$y = 9$$

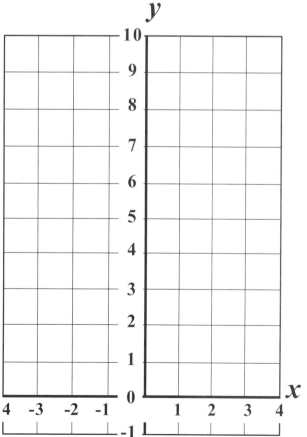

59

18. Simultaneous Equations

When two Equations which both have Variables have a Common Solution they are called Simultaneous Equations.

Example:

> Show there is a **Common Solution** to:
> $y = x - 1$ and $x + y = 6$

1. If we Substitute **4** for x:

$$y = x - 2$$
$$y = 4 - 2$$
$$y = 2$$

So $x = 4$ and $y = 2$

2. Now Substitute $x = 4$ and $y = 2$ into the other Equation:

$$x + y = 6$$
$$4 + 2 = 6$$

So $x = 4$ and $y = 2$ will satisfy both Equations.

At this level it is only necessary to solve Simultaneous Equations with the **Graphical Method** (using Graphs). This is done by drawing both Lines on the same Graph and finding where the two Lines Intersect. The **Solution to both Equations** is the **x and y Coordinates** at the **Point of Intersection**.

Example:

> Find the solution of the Simultaneous Equations: $2x + 3y = 12$ and $y = x - 1$ using the Graphical Method:

$$2x + 3y = 12$$

Use the Cover and Draw Method to draw the line:

Ignore the $3y$ | Ignore the $2x$

$2x + 3y = 12$ | $2x + 3y = 12$
$2x = 12$ | $3y = 12$
$x = 6$ | $y = 4$

$$y = x - 1$$

Create a Table of Values:

$y = x - 1$	$y = x - 1$
$y = 0 - 1$	$y = 4 - 1$
$y = -1$	$y = 3$

$y = x - 1$
$y = 2 - 1$
$y = 1$

x	0	2	4
y	-1	1	3

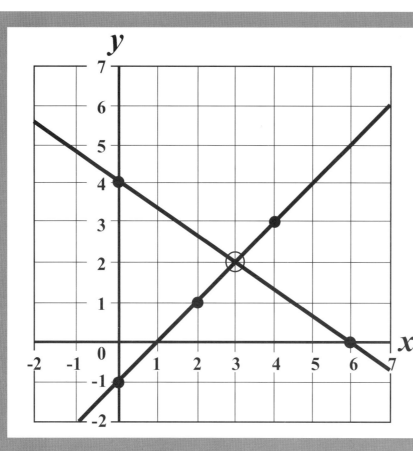

Once the lines have been Plotted, the point where they meet gives the Solution to the Equations.

The **Solution** to the Equations is:

$$x = 3$$
$$y = 2$$

Exercise 20: 27e   Answer the following:

9) Find the solution of the Simultaneous Equations:

$$y = 2x - 2 \qquad y - x = 1 \longrightarrow y = x + 1$$

Change this Equation to the standard format.

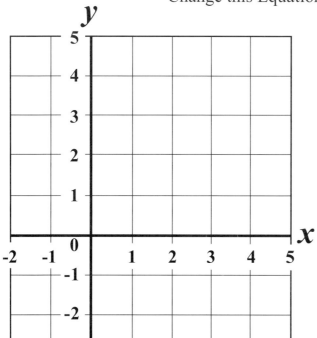

$y = 2x - 2$

x	0	1	2
y			

$y = x + 1$

x	0	1	2
y			

The Solution is

$x = $ ....

$y = $ ....

10) Find the Solution of the Simultaneous Equations:

$$2x + 3y = 6$$

$$x + y = 1$$

Use the Cover and Draw Method for both Equations:

The Solution is

x = ...

y = ...

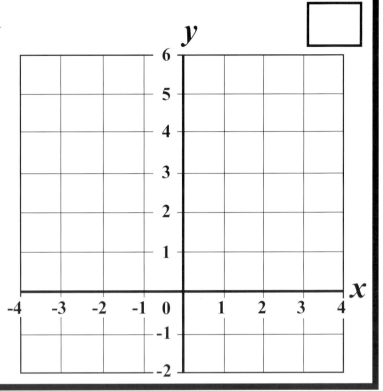

19. From Graphs to Equations

If a Graph is given and the **Equation of the Line** or the **Gradient** has to be identified, the best way to tackle it is by the **Gradient Intercept Method**.

Example: | What is the Equation of this Graph?

1. The **Gradient Intercept point** is **2**.

2. The **Gradient (x-coefficient)**:

$$= \frac{y\text{-step}}{x\text{-step}} = \frac{3}{1} = 3$$

3. The **Equation** can now be constructed: $y = 3x + 2$

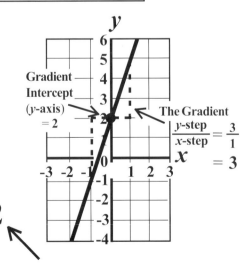

3 is the **Gradient** (steepness) of the Line or the **x-coefficient** on the **x-axis**. If it has a **Minus Value** the **Gradient is Negative**.

2 is the **Gradient Intercept** on the **y-axis**.

62

Exercise 20: 28 Find the Gradient of these Lines:

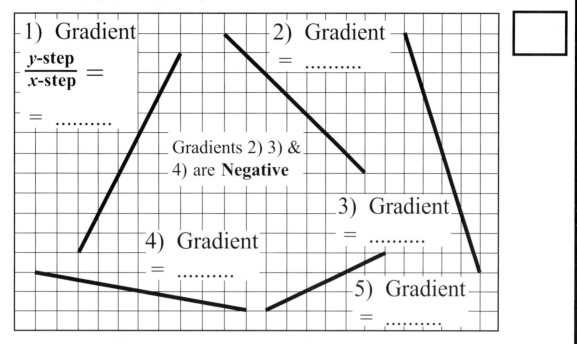

1) Gradient

$\dfrac{y\text{-step}}{x\text{-step}} =$

= ……….

2) Gradient

= ……….

Gradients 2) 3) &
4) are **Negative**

3) Gradient

= ……….

4) Gradient

= ……….

5) Gradient

= ……….

Find the Equation of the following Lines:

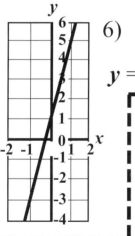

6)

$y =$ ……………

$y =$ ………………

8)

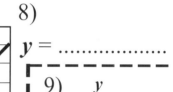

$y =$ ………………

9)

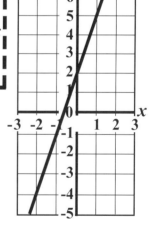

$y =$ ………………

7)

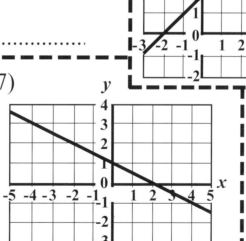

$y =$ ………………

Find with the **Cover and Draw Method**:

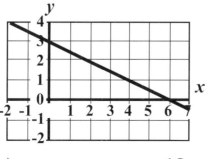

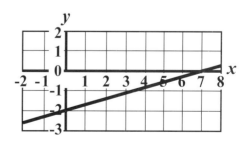

10) a) ……………… = **18**   b) ……………… = **14**

20. Algebra Problems

Exercise 20: 29 Answer the following:

1) A teacher asked a class to add up Algebraic Expressions:

2x + 3
x − 2
x + 6
x

3 pupils gave these answers:

Rikesh: **3x + 4**

Seneesh: **5x + 7**

Tim: **5x − 7**

a) Which pupil is correct?

....

b) If **x** is **3** what is the correct Expression worth?

....

---

2) A class bakes cakes. Andy bakes *c* cakes. Betty bakes **4** more cakes than Andy. Colin bakes **3** times as many cakes as Andy. Denise bakes **5** less cakes than Colin.

Name	Cakes
Andy	.....*c*........
Betty	a) ....
Colin	b) ....
Denise	c) ....

Write down on the table how many cakes each person bakes using Algebraic Formulae.

---

3) a) Fill out the Table of Values and Draw the Line for:

$$y = \frac{x}{3} - 1$$

It is necessary to choose values that will **divide by 3** so that a Table of Values can be easily created.

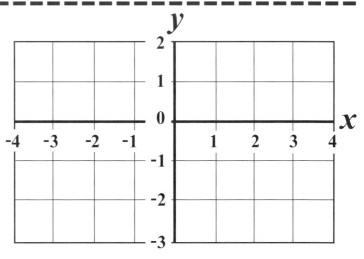

x	-3	0	3
y			

b) Is the Gradient of this Line Negative or Positive?

....

64

4) Jasmine and Anish play a game with counters. Each child starts with some bags of counters with **n** counters in each one. <u>The game is a tie</u> so Jasmine and Anish end up with the same number of counters.

Jasmine	**6** bags	lost **10** counters	**6n − 10**
Anish	**4** bags	won **6** counters	**4n + 6**

a) Write an Equation to find the value of **n**:

.... = ...   b) The value of **n** = ...

---

5) Some matchsticks were used to make up squares.

1 square   **2 squares**

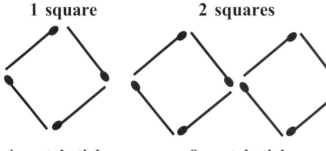

4 matchsticks   8 matchsticks

3 squares

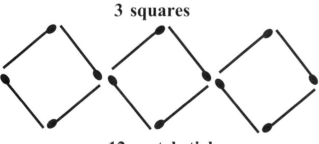

12 matchsticks

a) Write an Algebraic Rule for the number of matchsticks needed for each square pattern (**m** = **matchsticks** and **s** = **squares**).

m = ...

b) How many matches will be needed for **10** squares ....

---

6) Simplify these Expressions: a) $15y \div {}^{-}3$ = ...

b) $3(a + 2) + 2(a + b) - b$ = ...

c) $x - 4y - 3z - 3y + 5z + 2x$ = ...

---

7) Solve these Equations with the Balancing Method:

a) $4x + 4 = 10x - 8$ b) $5y - 6 = 15 - 2y$

x = ... y = ...

8) What are the Gradients of these Lines?

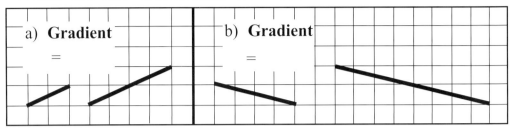

a) Gradient =

b) Gradient =

- -

9) Put the following numbers into this Function Machine:

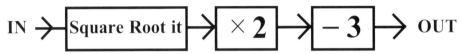

IN → Square Root it → × 2 → − 3 → OUT

Remember:
c) and d) require the Function Machine to be reversed.

| | IN | | | OUT |

a) **4** ⟶ ..... ⟶ ..... ⟶ .....

b) **9** ⟶ ..... ⟶ ..... ⟶ .....

c) ..... ⟵ ..... ⟵ ..... ⟵ **7**

d) ..... ⟵ ..... ⟵ ..... ⟵ **9**

- -

10) a) Draw Lines for these two Simultaneous Equations:

$$y = x - 2 \qquad x + y = 4$$

Fill in the Table of Values for: $y = x - 2$

x	0	2	4
y			

Use the Cover and Draw Method on:

$$x + y = 4$$

b) Where do the lines meet?

$x = $ .... $y = $ ....

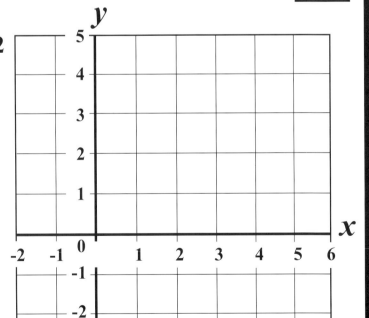

Answers

Chapter Twenty
Algebra

Exercise 20: 1

1) No   2) Yes   3) Yes
4) No   5) Yes   6) No
7) No   8) No   9) Yes
10) No

Exercise 20: 2

1) 14   2) -13
3) 10   4) -4
5) -3   6) -3
7) -5   8) 5
9) 7   10) 15

Exercise 20: 3

1) 12   2) -3
3) 4   4) -45
5) 21   6) -2
7) 54   8) -2
9) -4   10) -56

Exercise 20: 4

1) -39   2) 63
3) 5   4) -6
5) 18   6) -1
7) -224   8) -16
9) 2   10) 2

Exercise 20: 5

1) $3(3)$ or $-3(-3)$ 2) $2(3 + 4)$
3) $5(-3 + 7)$ 4) $4(4 + 5)$
5) $(3 \times 3) - (3 \times -5) = 24$
6) $(-3 \times 5) + (-3 \times 2) = -21$
7) $(-7 \times -5) + (-7 \times -2) = 49$
8) 10   9) 49   10) 54

Exercise 20: 6

1) 99   2) -6
3) 220   4) 0
5) 32   6) 6
7) 44   8) 12
9) 15   10) 25

Exercise 20: 7

1) 19   2) 29
3) 28   4) 21
5) 9   6) 85
7) 31   8) 81
9) 6   10) 26

Exercise 20: 8

1) $-$ 2) $\times$
3) $-$ 4) $\div$
5) $-$ 6) $-$
7) $+$ 8) $\div$
9) $\div$ 10) $\times$

Exercise 20: 9

1) 8   2) 20
3) 26   4) 165
5) 162   6) 13
7) 65   8) -91
9) 39   10) 104

Exercise 20: 10

1) 375   2) 9
3) 20   4) 24
5) 14   6) 15
7) 6   8) 8
9) 10   10) 14

Exercise 20: 11

1) $\times 11$ or -70 2) $\div 8$
3) $\times 3$ 4) $\div 50$ or -196
5) $+52$ 6) $\div 3$
7) $\times 2$
Rule is Add 35; Multiply by 2
8) 84   9) 9   10) 100

Exercise 20: 12

1) 5   2) x and $3y$
3) $3y$ 4) trinomial
5) unlike   6) unlike
7) like   8) unlike
9) unlike   10) like

Exercise 20: 13

1) $6x + 8$ 2) $6y - 5z$
3) $6y - 4z + 9$ 4) $-2a + 7b$
5) $x + 3yz$ 6) $-7y + z$
7) $xyz + 2xy$ 8) $2a - 2b + 4c$
9) $3x + 5y$ 10) $x - 4y + 3z$

Exercise 20: 14

1) $-35x$ 2) xy^2 3) $\frac{5x}{y}$
4) $2y$ 5) $7xy^2$ 6) y^3
7) $\frac{25yx^2}{4}$ 8) $\frac{24x}{-6} = -4x$
9) $2ab^2$ 10) $24xyz$

Exercise 20: 15

1) $4a + 12b$ 2) $5x - 15$
3) $xy + xz$ 4) $3a^2 - 2ab$
5) $-a^2 + ab$ 6) $6a + 8b$
7) $3a + 6 + 2a + 2b$
   $= 5a + 2b + 6$
8) $-x^2 + 5x + 2x - 2y$
   $= -x^2 + 7x - 2y$
9) $-4x - 20 + 2x - 6$
   $= -2x - 26$
10) $4a - 4b - 3a - 3b$
   $= a - 7b$

Answers

Exercise 20: 16
1) 32 2) 30
3) 39 4) -18
5) 14 6) -2
7) 26 8) -10
9) 30 10) 5

Exercise 20: 17
1) 3, 1 2) 625, 3125
3) 16, 18 4) -10, -15
5) 47, 76 6) 17, 19
7) 5, 2.5 8) 25, 36
9) 720 10) 27, 8

Exercise 20: 18a
1) a) 66 b) 96
2) a) 101 b) 157

Exercise 20: 18b
3) a) Rule is $2n + 1$
b) 14th is 29; 19th is 39
4) a) Rule is $4n - 1$
b) 15th is 59; 32nd is 127
5) a) Rule is $5n + 1$
b) 12th is 61; 16th is 81

Exercise 20: 18c
6) a) Rule is $5n + 2$
b) 18th is 92; 29th is 147
7) a) Rule is $6n - 1$
b) 16th is 95; 38th is 227
8) a) Rule is $6n + 6$
b) 15th is 96 matches
9) a) Rule is $3n$
b) 23rd is 69 matches
10) a) Rule is $3n + 1$
b) 46 matches

Exercise 20: 19a
1) $x = 3$ 2) $x = 3$
3) $x = 5$ 4) $x = 6$
5) $x = 4$

Exercise 20: 19b
6) $x = 2.2$ 7) $x = 2.7$
8) $x = 3.2$ 9) $x = 1.8$
10) $x = 3.6$

Exercise 20: 20a
1) $y = 3$ 2) $a = 30$
3) $b = 2$ 4) $a = 5$
5) $x = 64$

Exercise 20: 20b
6) $x = 32$ 7) $x = 4$
8) $a = 5$ 9) $y = 4$
10) $x = 2$

Exercise 20: 21a
1) $x = 7$ 2) $x = 9$
3) $x = 54$ 4) $y = 12$

Exercise 20: 21b
5) 2 6) 2
7) 2 8) 3

Exercise 20: 21c
9) a) $a = 4$
b) $21 = 21$
yes it balances
10) a) $x = 2$
b) $-1 = -1$
Yes it balances

Exercise 20: 22a
1) 20°C 2) 4°C
3) 15°C 4) -11°C
5) 27°C

Exercise 20: 22b
6) 70°F 7) 61°F
8) 36°F 9) 14°F
10) 81°F

Exercise 20: 23
1) $n + 7$ 2) $\frac{b}{8}$
3) $2y + x$ 4) $c - 7$
5) $4x - 3$ 6) $y - 5$
7) $\frac{5 + n}{y}$ 8) $\frac{3n - 6}{4}$
9) $\frac{x + 5}{y}$ 10) $\frac{p}{2} - r$

Exercise 20: 24a
1) $\frac{y}{5}$ 2) $9x$
3) $50x + 50y$ 4) $\frac{m + e + s}{3}$
5) $52x + 12y$

Exercise 20: 24b
6) a) $\frac{50}{x}$ b) $\frac{50}{x} \times 30$
7) a) $y = \frac{x^2}{2} + 3$ b) 11
8) a) $2x + 9 = 27$ b) 9

Exercise 20: 24c
9) a) $2x + 4 = x + 14$
   b) $x = 10$
10) a) $4y - 9 = y + 15$
   b) $y = 8$

Exercise 20: 25a
1) $x - 11$
2) a) $r + 10 = 40$ b) 30
3) $x = 5$

Exercise 20: 25b
4) $3x + 3y + 3z$
5) a) $2n^2$ b) $6n$
6) $2a + 2b$

Exercise 20: 25c
7) a) $C = 1200 + 160h$
   b) £21.60
8) a) $6s + 3$ b) $s = 17$
9) a) $4x + 16$
   b) $x = 2$; Equation is:
$4x + 16 = 10x + 4$
10) a) £24 b) $y = 30$

Answers

Exercise 20: 26a

1)
Line A

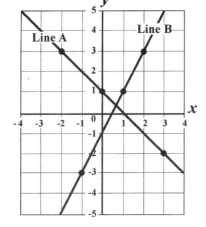

2) Line B

x	2	1	-1
y	3	1	-3

Exercise 20: 26b

3) $y = 2$ 4) $y = x$

5) $x = -3$ 6) $y = -x$

Exercise 20: 26c

7) $y = 3x$

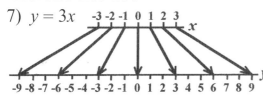

8) $y = x - 3$

x	-2	-1	0	1	2	3
y	-5	-4	-3	-2	-1	0

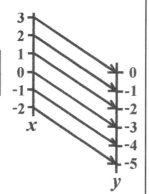

9) $y = x^2$

x	0	1	2	3	4
y	0	1	4	9	16

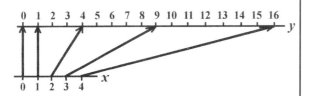

10) $y = 3x - 1$

x	-2	-1	0	1	2
y	-7	-4	-1	2	5

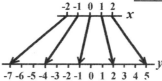

Exercise 20: 27a

1) $y = 3x - 2$

a)

x	0	1	2
y	-2	1	4

b) Positive

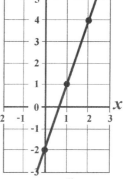

2) $y = \frac{x}{2} - 1$

a)

x	-4	0	2
y	-3	-1	0

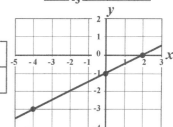

b) Positive

Exercise 20: 27b

3) $3x - 5y = 15$

a)

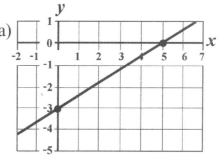

b) Positive

4) $2x + 5y = -10$

a)

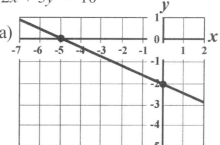

b) Negative

Answers

Exercise 20: 27c

5) $y = -2x$ a)

b) Negative

6) $y = \frac{x}{2} + 2$

a)

b) Positive

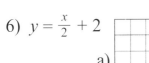

Exercise 20: 27d

7) $y = x^2 + 1$

x	-3	-2	-1	0	1	2	3
y	10	5	2	1	2	5	10

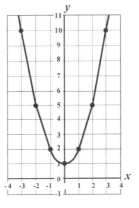

8) $y = x^2$

x	-3	-2	-1	0	1	2	3
y	9	4	1	0	1	4	9

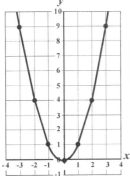

Exercise 20: 27e

9) $y = 2x - 2$

x	0	1	2
y	-2	0	2

$y = x + 1$

x	0	1	2
y	1	2	3

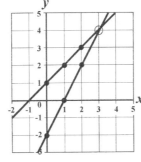

The solution is $x = 3$; $y = 4$

10)

The solution is
$x = -3$; $y = 4$

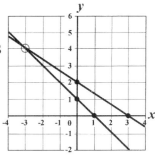

Exercise 20: 28

1) 2   2) -1   3) -3   4) $-\frac{1}{5}$

5) $\frac{1}{2}$ 6) $y = 4x + 1$

7) $y = -\frac{1}{2}x + 1$ 8) $y = x + 2$

9) $y = 3x + 2$ 10) a) $3x + 6y = 18$

b) $2x - 7y = 14$

Exercise 20: 29

1) a) Seneesh with $5x + 7$ b) 22

2) a) $c + 4$ b) $3c$ c) $3c - 5$

3) $y = \frac{x}{3} - 1$

a)
x	-3	0	3
y	-2	-1	0

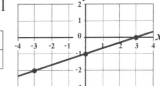

b) Positive

4) a) $6n - 10 = 4n + 6$

b) $n = 8$

5) a) $4s$

b) 40 matches

6) a) $-5y$ b) $5a + b + 6$

c) $3x - 7y + 2z$

7) a) $x = 2$ b) $y = 3$

8) a) $\frac{1}{2}$ b) $-\frac{1}{4}$

9) a) 1   b) 3

c) 25   d) 36

10) a) $y = x - 2$

x	0	2	4
y	-2	0	2

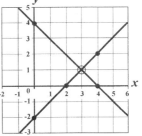

b) The lines meet
at $x = 3$; $y = 1$

PROGRESS CHARTS

20. ALGEBRA

Marks

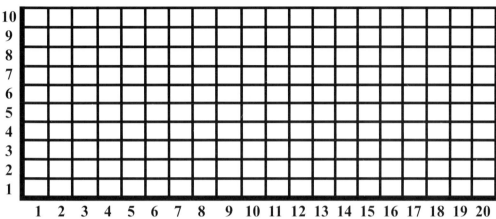

1 2 3 4 5 6 7 8 9 10 11 12 13 14 15 16 17 18 19 20
Exercises

Marks

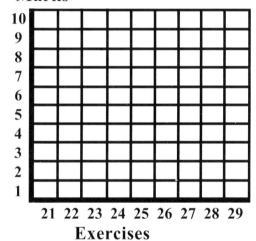

21 22 23 24 25 26 27 28 29
Exercises

Total Mark

Percentage

%

CERTIFICATE
OF
ACHIEVEMENT
(Sixth)

This certifies...............................

has completed **Maths Book Six** successfully.

Overall Percentage
Score Achieved.

%

Comment....................................

....

Signed ....
(teacher/parent/guardian)

Date ....